Social Stratification in the United States

THE AMERICAN PROFILE POSTER

NEW EDITION

Stephen J. Rose

THE NEW PRESS
NEW YORK

Requests for permission to reproduce selections from this book should be mailed to:
Permissions Department, The New Press, 120 Wall Street, 31st floor,
New York, NY 10005.

Originally published in the United States by The New Press, New York, 1992
This edition published by The New Press, New York, 2014
Distributed by Perseus Distribution

ISBN 978-1-62097-005-8 (pbk with poster)
CIP data available

The New Press publishes books that promote and enrich public discussion and
understanding of the issues vital to our democracy and to a more equitable world.
These books are made possible by the enthusiasm of our readers; the support of a
committed group of donors, large and small; the collaboration of our many
partners in the independent media and the not-for-profit sector; booksellers,
who often hand-sell New Press books; librarians; and above all by our authors.

www.thenewpress.com

Book design and composition by Lovedog Studio
This book was set in Sabon

Printed in the United States of America

2 4 6 8 10 9 7 5 3 1

Contents

Acknowledgments

MANY TEACHERS AND COMMENTATORS HAVE used various visual images to portray disparities in the distribution of income in the United States—for example, a marching band that takes an hour to pass the viewing stand, or the Eiffel Tower. In the early 1970s, sociologist Jan Houbolt solicited the graphic assistance of Dennis Livingston to create a 100-figure chart with managers, teachers, carpenters, and other occupational categories. The purpose was to personalize mathematical relations that students often comprehended only vaguely.

In 1978 Livingston and I expanded this initial idea to create a statistically accurate 1,000-figure portrayal of the American social structure. With money raised from friends, the Social Graphics Company was formed to produce the original *Social Stratification in the United States* poster and guidebook. After the first edition and a 1980 reprint were sold out, a new edition was created in 1983. Kathryn Shagas took over the artistic presentation and redesigned the icons and layout. Interest and sales continued, leading Tom Engelhardt, then an editor at Pantheon Books, to commission a 1986 update with a changed title, *The American Profile Poster.*

In 1992, the next updated edition was published by The New Press, and the original title was restored. After updates in 2000 and 2007, this poster and booklet represent the seventh edition of the original 1978 concept. The poster continues to represent the clearest and most succinct picture of America's social structure, providing a basis for tracking social change over the past thirty-five years.

Over the years, many people have graciously supported the concept and the execution of these and related poster-books. To the original twenty-five "investors" and many friends, heartfelt thanks are due. Earlier versions of the poster benefited greatly from the input of Barbara Koeppel, Nancy Hartsock, and Tom Engelhardt. David Wright at Wichita State University was responsible for preparing data from the computer tapes of the 1980 and 2013 Current Population Surveys (the ongoing yearly census study of 60,000 to 80,000 households). Finally, I wish to thank Brian Mulligan, who prepared this edition of the poster, and Jed Bickman of The New Press, who shepherded the current version of the poster-book to completion.

It is interesting to compare the original and current procedures used to create the poster. In 1975 the data were tabulated from published census reports using a hand calculator without a printer; when a total did not correspond correctly, an entire series of numbers had to be reentered. To produce the artwork for the poster, sketches of the figures were made to create rubber block stamps. These stamps were inked and manually pressed to a white board, and marking pens were applied to tracing paper to add the coloration. Changes required white-outs and cut-outs. Finally, the artwork was sent to Florida to create the four-color-process negatives.

From the standpoint of 2014, these procedures seem archaic. The current data were tabulated directly off computer files. The output was converted into spreadsheets and sent from Wichita on CD-ROMs. Once the characteristics of the one thousand adults were assigned, the artwork for the poster was created on a desktop computer. The icons were created as computer images that could be easily manipulated. The figures and other poster elements were assembled in a desktop drawing program, and colors were assigned. Finally, a color separator produced film negatives for printing directly from the computer file.

All of these advances have made the product look more professional (although some prefer the quirky hand-drawn nature of the first edition) and easier to manipulate in preparing final production. Nonetheless, having one thousand figures represent 200 million people is a difficult challenge that requires the laborious task of satisfying multiple conditions at the same time. This effort of creation and manipulation has not changed over time, showing that the essence of any good idea or product is still human ingenuity.

Introduction

THE PURPOSE OF THIS POSTER AND BOOKLET IS to show, in an easily accessible way, how various groups in the American population are faring in terms of several social indicators. Much of this information is discussed in the media and in classrooms. However, the numbers, percentages, and median figures can be confusing and hard to relate to one another. The poster is an attempt to overcome this problem by presenting the data in a single visual picture. In this form, the relationships of income, wealth, and education to such variables as race, gender, and household type are visible at a glance.

One of the original purposes of the poster was to show the vast differences in incomes across the American population. In the first edition that came out in 1978, the following statement appeared on the poster: "The 1,124 families who declared over $1 million on their tax would be thirteen stories above the poster." The comparable statement on this poster is: "To depict the 12,000 households who declared more than $10 million on their tax returns in 2011 would require a poster fifteen stories high." Finally, the number of tax returns of at least $1 million ($340,000 in 1979 dollars) has risen to 301,000.

Even though prices have nearly tripled and population has grown by 60 percent, this rise in income among the superwealthy has been one of the oddest features of the past thirty years. The pay packages of top corporate executives, financial professionals, and entertainment stars in the arts and athletics have been mind-boggling and was one of the rallying cries of the Occupy movement—"we are the 99 percent." While the Occupy movement has lost some of its steam, the surprise best seller in May 2014 was Thomas Piketty's *Capital in the Twenty-First Century*, which focused on the share of income and wealth of the top 1 percent,[1] Yet, as will be shown below, the inequality that looked large in the 1970s has gotten worse, and it involves more than just the top 1 percent.

The poster employs many graphic elements—icons, placement, and color—to present a large quantity of information. Each icon (or figure) represents 200,000 people. There are separate icons for each type of household status: single men and single women (without dependents), married couples with both partners present (with or without other dependents), and single men and women with dependents (primarily children) but no spouse present.

Only adults who are responsible for their own well-being are included. This means that children over eighteen, parents, or other relatives living with a couple or single head of household are excluded. Roommates are considered two separate households, but cohabitors are treated as married.

Because of the vast differences between the richest and poorest Americans, the icons are distributed along three separate income lines. First, the graph with the largest icons, on the left side of the poster, shows the distribution of the population by

1. Published by The Belknap Press of Harvard University Press, Cambridge, Massachusetts: 2014.

combined household incomes (from all sources and all family members and before taxes but after cash government payments—e.g., social security, unemployment insurance, etc.) up to $150,000. Only 88 percent of the population fits on this graph. Second, the income graph with the white background and very small icons presents the entire distribution from incomes of zero (usually due to business losses) to one million. And third, the chart on the far right with medium-sized icons is an enlargement of those with incomes between $150,000 and $400,000.

Also included to the left of the complete income line (the income figures with the white background) are rows of green dollars to show the average level of wealth of households at different levels of income. Wealth consists of assets held rather than wages and salaries. Most people's wealth consists of tangible things—houses, cars, consumer durables, and so on. However, the bulk of the richest people's wealth is composed of financial assets, such as stocks, bonds, insurance policies, and the businesses they own.

For the first time, the color coding of the icons indicates educational categories rather than occupations (professional, clerical, unskilled blue collar, etc.), if employed, or one of four nonemployed conditions: housewife (less than 1 percent of nonemployed men describe themselves as "keeping house"), retired, unemployed but actively seeking employment, or not in the labor force but not actively seeking employment (for example, on welfare, disabled, homeless, and so on).

The shift to education represents the rising importance of formal schooling in determining occupation and incomes. The practice of promoting from within to fill top jobs has been largely replaced by separate recruiting requirements based largely on educational credentials. While there have been exceptions, such as Bill Gates, Michael Dell, and Steve Jobs, 92 percent of Fortune 500 company leaders have a BA, and half have a graduate degree. Almost the same ratios apply to members of Congress, and the last president not to have a BA was Harry Truman (and he finished high school at the beginning of the 1900s). Actually, since Richard Nixon, every president received his undergraduate degree from a highly selective university.

Race is also depicted graphically. Non-Hispanic white people have white clothes and faces. Non-Hispanic African Americans, Hispanics (primarily people from Central and South America), and people of other races (e.g., Asians and Native Americans) have dark clothes and faces; diagonal, horizontal, or vertical stripes are also used to identify these three racial/ethnic categories. Hispanics are not in fact a racial category, but they face discrimination and have income profiles much closer to African Americans than to white Americans. This distinction is accepted in public policy—for example, in affirmative action guidelines—and thus merits separate treatment on the poster, especially since Hispanics are a growing share of the population.

Finally, the world is getting more complex, making necessarily simplifying assumptions less tenable. In particular, there are no gay couples represented on the poster, even though their numbers are large enough to represent ten figures on the poster. Similarly, there are no interracial couples because the various combinations are too many to present in concert with incomes and educational levels.

The data used to create this poster are derived from a census survey conducted in March 2013. This survey is part of an ongoing annual study of social and economic conditions and is much more timely than the decennial census. Because the overall relationships of income, household formation, and occupation change slowly (especially during the slow growth that has occurred at the tail end of the Great Recession), the presentation of the poster should remain accurate for many more years with only some small adjustment to reflect monetary inflation.

From a distance, the flows of colors and the overall shape of the graph tell us a lot about our income distribution. As one moves closer, individual families and the differences between them appear. The tables and graphs in this booklet complement the poster by presenting a complete mathematical breakdown of each of the statistical relationships. These are the building blocks from which the poster was constructed. In many cases, current conditions are compared to 1979 data (the year of the original poster). These differences reveal the changing nature of the social landscape in America. In particular, attention is paid to the widely used concept of "middle class." Often, people use this term too broadly and include virtually all of the population. The poster and accompanying data allow the viewer to investigate what various components of the middle class have in common and the ways in which they differ. The purpose is to stimulate discussion about these important questions rather than provide "answers."

Those who have seen earlier versions of this poster will note that the shape has changed a little bit. The share of those with relatively low incomes (at or just a bit above the poverty line) has remained constant, the bulge in the middle has flattened a bit, and a few more people have joined the "upper middle class." Thus, the growth over the last twenty years (of about 1 percent a year per person after inflation) has been unequally distributed. Those at the bottom have not seen any gains; most in the middle have had modest economic gains in their standard of living; and the lion's share of the gains have gone to those in the top third of the income ladder. A fuller description of these developments will be presented below.

At the end of the text are three appendixes. The first appendix contains fourteen tables that show the exact distribution of icons on the poster. The second appendix presents suggestions for classroom use. The final appendix is a listing of other works published by the author on topics covered in the booklet.

A Note on Statistics and Reading Charts

NUMBERS ARE USED CONSTANTLY IN PUBLIC debate, lending a certain air of finality and definitiveness. Many people are not taken in by this ploy and are suspicious of anyone using numbers; others retreat in awe. Everyone knows how confusing it is when something they believe to be true is "refuted" by someone using statistics.[2] What are they to do—believe their instinct or their opponent's argument? Fortunately, they are saved many times by their belief in the quip: "There are liars, dirty liars, and people who use statistics."

In frustration, many people shy away from data-driven arguments and turn to anecdotes. I am sure that you have heard the one about your friend's feisty ninety-year-old grandmother who smoked three packs of cigarettes a day her whole adult life, drank like a fish, and had a cholesterol level of five hundred. And so? This is an example of the little jibes that people take at experts and of the lack of confidence in the use of statistics. Because not every single smoker dies at sixty does not mean that smoking is not bad for your health.

Suspicion of statistics is unfortunate because quantitative analysis can be a powerful tool in presenting and understanding complicated relationships. Part of the problem is "mathophobia." But it is also true that statistics can be manipulated. For instance, a demographic statistic is usually present-ed as "x percent of the y population fits the relevant criteria." Whoever defines x and y has tremendous power over the impression created by that data.

Let us look at a few examples to highlight this point. A television commercial proclaims that two-thirds of TV engineers prefer TV sets made by Brand A, while a competing commercial assures us that two-thirds of TV engineers own Brand B sets. These assertions can both be true because they address different questions—preference and ownership. Company B may be a broadcasting company that produces TV sets and sells them to its engineers at a deep discount; so, these engineers may own brand B but prefer another. Another simple explanation may be that Brand B is cheaper.

Another more complex example involves making international comparisons. In 2000, I spent a couple of months in Strasbourg, France, while a friend was spending a month in Paris. He thought that the quality of life was higher in France than in America for middle-class families. He reasoned that the quality of goods was higher (the beloved corner bakery shop), no one had to worry about health insurance, the public transportation system was much better, there were more interesting places to visit, the workweek was shorter, and the workers took longer vacations.

I argued that there was no way to compare the two countries because they had different priorities. Yes, the French worked fewer hours, but this meant that shops were closed from noon on Saturday through Monday morning. Yes, public transportation was better, but the roads in the

2. The way in which the mass media present this debate makes matters worse. Reporters are taught to withhold judgment and be the neutral arbiter presenting all opinions. They go to great effort to find alternative voices, even if they are not nearly as credible, in their desire to be "balanced."

Statistical Measures

Often, a single number is used to represent the conditions of a group; for example, the typical administrative assistant makes x dollars. Clearly some make less and others earn more, but we use a single number to represent all administrative assistants. There are various ways of communicating what is "typical." The average, or *mean*, salary is determined by adding the salaries of all administrative assistants and dividing by the number of administrative assistants. The *median* salary, by contrast, is derived by ranking all administrative assistants in order of their income and finding the salary at which half the administrative assistants make more and half make less. In other words, the median value tells you the salary of the one in the middle. In general, the average tends to be higher than the median because the values at the high end of the distribution raise the mean but do not affect the median.

The mean and median are measures of central tendency—that is, they are different ways of describing the most common feature of a population. Sometimes, however, it is useful to obtain a more complete picture by looking at the status of people who are at different points along the pay scale—for example, the poorest 20 percent or the richest 5 percent. In order to do this, all observations must be ranked according to the appropriate measure, be it height or income. One example that many students are familiar with is their SAT scores. These are reported as a raw score for each test (e.g., 650) and a percentile level (88th percentile). The percentile score reveals how you did relative to everyone else taking the exam. Often, when reporting about income distribution, analysts divide the population into five groups, or *quintiles*, and report the average income of each. This convention is used to more fully describe a diverse population.

A population is often divided into different groups or subpopulations. Race and occupation are two factors used in constructing the poster. Each group (e.g., African Americans or farmers) is reported as a percentage of the whole. More detailed analysis separates this part into yet smaller units, which are reported as percentages of the subpopulation. Given that a family has many characteristics—income, occupation, race, and the number, gender, and age of its members, among others—a variety of information can be reported about it. Each value identified with this family refers it in a different way to various segments of the overall population with which it shares something in common.

cities were very narrow and hard to navigate; furthermore, the narrow streets meant that cars were often parked on the sidewalks. An additional hassle of car ownership was the $8 price for a gallon of gas, decreasing the attractiveness of light trucks, minivans, and SUVs.

Most of France was a tourist destination, with quaint buildings everywhere. It was fun to visit and take in the sights. But a lot of apartment buildings did not have elevators; having more than one bathroom per apartment was a rarity; and the average living space was a little more than half the size of a typical American house. Furthermore, the French watched dubbed American movies, and mainly had talking heads and variety shows on nightly television.

When comparing living conditions in western Europe to those in the United States, many researchers say it is better to be rich in America (because of the very high taxes on wealthy people in Europe) and poor in Europe (because of the extensive social safety net). No one really knows how to accurately compare the living conditions of those in the middle.

My own take on the comparison is that one can't make it. I feel that if you plopped some American suburbanites in the outskirts of Strasbourg, they would feel uncomfortable and miss much of their American life. Conversely, members of the French middle class moving to America would also experience their share of culture shock. The bottom line is that these two societies have high standards of living and choose to live quite differently. To the degree that someone has tried to quantify living standards, the Organisation for Economic Cooperation and Development reports that in terms of "purchasing power parity," Americans have a significantly higher standard of living.

Another crucial issue is making comparisons over time, which requires adjusting for inflation. The Consumer Price Index (CPI) is used to separate purely monetary changes from the underlying "real" differences in living standards. It is difficult to construct the CPI, and the government agency in charge of constructing it (the Bureau of Labor Statistics) is constantly updating its procedures.

In addition to inflation, the size of households has shrunk as more people live alone as singles and there are fewer married couples and more single parents. In determining poverty, there isn't a single income cutoff but a separate one for each sized household. This approach is based on the premise that two can't live as cheaply as one, but it doesn't cost twice as much because of economies of scale (e.g,, only one housing unit is needed).

A final crucial issue about living standards is that the definition of income in government surveys is limited to cash payments from earnings, interest payments, dividends, pensions, and government transfers such as Social Security and unemployment insurance. Economists prefer a broader definition of income to include all factors that impact your economic status in a year. They would include the value of employer-paid benefits (as health care costs have risen, the value of this benefit has grown substantially), the value of noncash public transfers (e.g., the value of Medicare, Medicaid, food stamps, and housing vouchers), and the appreciation of all financial assets whether sold or not. The difference in these two approaches is substantial

when trying to determine growth over time: using a comprehensive measure of well-being adjusted for household size, the Congressional Budget Office found the median real income grew by 35 percent from 1979 to 2007. By contrast, the Census Report on Income found just a 13 percent real gain at the median.

Clearly, this can be confusing to the layperson, and it is tempting to decide that the statistics are meaningless and we will never know the truth. But then where are we left? Instead, we should try to find the answer that is consistent with as many other measures as possible. No one can prove that theirs is *the* final and right answer. However, combining data from a variety of approaches very often allows a general consensus to emerge.

In general, when making data-driven statements, we are trying to highlight the independent effect of a specific variable. In the physical sciences, laboratory experiments and random assignment trials provide the best setting to isolate the effect of a single variable on a relevant outcome measure. With few exceptions, these options are not available for social science research. The most important things to keep in mind when presented with a social science data analysis are:

- **Unit of analysis**—Is it the family, individual workers, a specific type of worker?

- **Classification**—How is each category defined, especially since subgroups are usually very important to the analysis?

- **Reference point**—Comparisons are usually made with one group being compared and contrasted with another group.

Measurement of changes over time requires adjusting for the general rate of inflation. It turns out that economies function more smoothly with a small level of inflation. Over time, this compounds, and it is important to use "inflation-adjusted" comparisons rather than simply the prices that exist (economists call this the difference between real and nominal dollar amounts). Making the appropriate inflation adjustments is tricky, and the

Data Sources

Social science statistics come from a variety of sources, with the most common source being surveys of 20,000 to 150,000 respondents. This may surprise many people who think that there are massive data sets with information of all kinds about most people. After all, there are credit agency reports, tax records, Social Security account information, medical records, marriage licenses, and myriad other collections of information about us. Put them all together and you should be able to know most everything about everyone.

Fortunately, this is not the case! Most government agencies have strong protections about using their data for purposes other than what is necessary to perform their function. These data cannot be shared, and they are not linked with one another in a master data set. Marketers have created various synthetic data sets that try to combine information from many sources. But they are not able to get actual matches of information from different sources about the same person. As a result, from time to time, we hear about the credit card offered to Fido Smith, the loyal dog of the Smith family.

Social scientists, then, are forced to rely on specialized surveys. For example, the official unemployment rate is announced on the first Friday of every month. A common misperception is that this figure is based on a count of people receiving unemployment compensation checks. This is not the case; the unemployed include all those who are seeking a job, rather than just those who are getting benefits (in fact, less than 40 percent of the unemployed receive benefits). Instead the unemployment rate is derived from a monthly survey of 80,000 adults.

The long form of the decennial census is an excellent source of information, but it is only collected once every ten years. To provide more timely information, the U.S. government started the monthly Current Population Survey (CPS) in 1964 (replacing a shorter survey that had been started in 1948). Most of the articles you read about earnings, employment, and family status come from this survey and its various monthly supplements.

The American government has actually been an international leader in recognizing the importance of publicly available, accurate information. In addition to the CPS, in 2003 the Census Bureau began conducting the American Community Survey to provide current social information at the state and community levels. There are also many specialized surveys that deal with health, education, and employer practices.

Surveys are widely used because researchers have become confident in their ability to collect limited data that reflects the conditions of the entire population. Sampling statisticians have developed techniques to construct samples that are both cost-efficient and accurate. Some researchers have such confidence in this approach that they suggested that surveys would provide a better estimate of inner-city populations for the 2000 census than direct counts.

This counterintuitive proposal appalled many people who felt that a real count had to be better than a limited count. In general, this principle is true, but what about conditions in which you can't get a real count? Virtually everyone involved in collecting past censuses agreed that it was hard to reach all inner-city residents and that this population had historically been undercounted. So, the choice was not really between a census and survey but between two imperfect ways of estimating a figure when people were often not available to be counted. Statisticians argued that you could target your resources to get a few counts right and then

(Continued)

use the data obtained from this limited, high-intensity census to estimate the populations in many other cities. Not surprisingly, the statisticians lost, because the politicians and public did not have as much confidence in survey techniques as they did.

One last thing about surveys needs to be noted. Most surveys are taken at a single point in time and ask about current conditions and income or earnings over the past year. These cross-sectional or snapshot surveys are more useful in describing the state of the overall economy than they are in describing individual conditions. The reason for this is that people's conditions change over time. In particular, there is a life-cycle effect of school, entry-level jobs, career and advancement, and retirement.

In fact, not all issues of mobility and opportunity can be addressed with cross-sectional surveys. As an alternative, longitudinal or panel surveys follow the same people over many years. Keeping in contact with these people is a huge undertaking and makes longitudinal surveys much more expensive than single-shot surveys. Therefore, they tend to be smaller and there are fewer of them. But they will be cited in the ensuing text because of the richness of the data that they provide.

Bureau of Labor Statistics has changed its methods several times over the last thirty years. This creates the odd situation in which the preferred inflation adjustment (the CPS-U-RS) is different from the "official" CPS-U. This opens the door to some results showing a much worse economic performance than reported elsewhere because they use the incorrect inflation adjustment.

When using a quantitative approach it is important to specify if the comparison of two groups is done on the basis of averages, distributions, or relative standing.

While using statistics can be a tricky undertaking, if you know how the question is being defined and whether the measures being used are accurate and appropriate to the task, you will be well equipped to evaluate what is happening. The next time someone rattles off a number to prove a point, don't tune out and feel overwhelmed. Instead, think for a moment about whom and what is being counted, clarify the source of the information and the definitions being used, and make up your own mind about the accuracy of the numbers.

Household Characteristics

IN THIS WORK THE FOCUS IS ON ADULTS WHO are responsible for their own well-being. This includes all married persons living together in one household (with and without dependents), single men and women living on their own, and single parents with children but no spouse. Adults not represented include those over eighteen years of age who are still living with their parents, elderly people living with relatives, and people in institutions such as the armed forces, prisons, and mental hospitals.

Table 1 presents the breakdown of the population represented by one thousand icons on the poster. Each icon, representing 200,000 people, or 0.1 percent of the nondependent adult population, stands for either husbands, wives,[3] single men, single women, or single men or women with dependents but no spouse (also called male- and female-headed households).

In relationship with the 1979 poster, the current one has seventy-six fewer couples even though there are nearly fifty icons representing unmarried couples living together. Most of the gains were in the share of single people without dependents. Today, single young adulthood apart from one's family is considered a normal—even cherished—stage in one's life. The other large group of singles

is the elderly (primarily women) who have chosen independence over family ties, spawning the explosion of retirement communities. In not all cases, however, has this decision been voluntary, as adult children are either unwilling or unable to take in elderly parents. By contrast, in Japan over half of elderly widows live with their children. As a result of these changes, the United States has one of the highest levels of single-person households in the world.

By contrast, the share of single mothers has only increased modestly, while the number of single fathers has doubled in size but from a very low base. It is important to note, however, that female-headed families were actually not that uncommon in the 1940s and 1950s. Of white families in 1940, 8 percent were headed by women without a spouse present. Today, that figure is 12 percent. The change is much more dramatic among black families. In 1940, 16 percent of black families were headed by a female; today 42 percent are. Another important aspect of this change is the incre asing proportion who were never married. In the past, single-female-headed households were often caused by a husband's death or abandonment. Finally, it should be noted that women represent 58 percent of single-adult households. This reflects the following: (1) women are far more likely to be single parents; (2) women live longer than men, with single elderly women outnumbering comparable men by a three-to-one margin; and (3) many more men than women are in the armed forces or in prisons, and therefore excluded from the data.

3. We include the 14 million cohabiting adults who are not married but live with an adult of the opposite sex. This represents 7 percent of all intact husband-wife couples, and fully one-half of cohabitors have a child present. By contrast, in 1979, only 3 percent of couples were unmarried cohabitors and only 25 percent had children present.

THE RISE OF SINGLE-ADULT HOUSEHOLDS, BY ICONS ON THE POSTER

	1979	2013	Change
Couples (married and cohabiting)	756	680	- 76
Single men	72	109	+ 37
Single women	94	114	+ 20
Male head	13	26	+ 13
Female head	65	71	+ 6

Despite this shift to single-adult households, nearly 70 percent of nondependent adults live in intact husband-wife couples (including cohabitors). The media gives so much attention to divorce and nontraditional living arrangements that most people expect this number to be much lower. In fact, most single women are elderly widows, while young adults tend to remain single and living away from their parents for only a few years before finding a mate. Divorce has become much more common, but, in most cases, is followed by remarriage, in a kind of serial monogamy. The result is often a "blended family," in which children may live with stepparents, half siblings, and stepsiblings.

As was noted, adult children living with their parents are excluded from this analysis, and some might think that this adds a bias because of the many stories on adult children returning to their parents' homes. As Table 2 shows, the number of adult children living with parents is up but not that significantly (about 8 percentage points for people in their twenties). The cases of children older than twenty-seven and older parents living with their adult children are rarer (in the middle single digits of percentages of each population).

Race/Ethnicity

The race/ethnicity of the population represented by each icon is shown in Table 3. It is important to note that the definition of race is not clear-cut.

Studies of African Americans, for instance, reveal that well over half have some European or "white American" ancestry. Similarly, Hispanics[4] come from many different races and some are mixtures of different races. Finally, the category of "other nonwhites" comprises primarily people of Asian descent, secondarily Native Americans, and some people who report that they are multiracial. All of these groups have to be combined in order to have a large enough population to accurately allocate each icon by gender, household status, income, and education.

The number of icons representing non-Hispanic whites has declined by 164 with most of the change due to the increased number of Hispanic and other races. By contrast, the number of African American icons increased modestly from 96 to 108. As has been widely noted, the number of Hispanics in the United States has surpassed the number of African Americans. The final race/ethnicity category is "other races," which is composed primarily of people from Asia (e.g., Chinese, Indian, Vietnamese, Korean, and Cambodian). There has been an explosion of the number of Asians in America over the last thirty years, and, as result, the number of icons of other races has grown from 14 in 1979 to 69 in the current poster.

Going forward, it is expected that the number of nonwhites (including white Hispanics) will con-

4. Government reports often refer to this group as "being of Hispanic origin" and include people of European descent. The vast majority of this category was born in, or can be traced back to, Central or South America.

TABLE 2:
HOUSEHOLD STATUS OF TWENTY-YEAR-OLDS

	Married or single parent (%)	Single or with roommate (%)	Living with parents or relatives (%)
Early Twenties (22–24)			
2014	21	31	48
2004	30	30	41
1995	33	27	40
1985	38	22	40
Midtwenties (25–27)			
2014	37	35	28
2004	50	28	22
1995	51	26	23
1985	59	22	20

TABLE 3:
GROWING RACIAL AND ETHNIC DIVERSITY

	1979	2013	Change
Non-Hispanic whites	852	688	-164
African Americans	96	108	+ 12
Hispanics	38	135	+ 97
Other races and multiple races	14	69	+ 55

tinue to increase and become a majority at some point in the 2040s. These populations are younger and their birth rates are slightly higher than that of whites. In many elementary and high school districts in our large metropolitan areas, over half the student body is nonwhite of various backgrounds. It is not unusual for some school districts to have students with more than fifty different languages spoken at home.

The explosion of nonwhite students has occurred while the birth rates of these populations have been

5. This reduction in family size is common to all the advanced industrial countries; indeed, several European countries and Japan have had negative population growth over the last decade because the number of deaths is outstripping the number of births.

falling.[5] Contrary to popular belief, the fall in birth rates has been greatest among teenage girls, especially African Americans. In 1960, the birth rate per 1,000 women 15 to 19 years old was 158 children for African Americans and 79 for whites. In 2010, teenage non-Hispanic whites had 24 births per 1,000 while African Americans and Hispanics had rates of 52 and 56. One of the main reasons for this decline is that young people are marrying and having children later. Unfortunately, this means that most teen births now occur out of wedlock (89 percent of blacks and 39 percent of whites) with all the accompanying problems that result.

One of the big differences for African Americans is that they are much less likely to be in a husband-wife couple. As Table 4 shows, all of the

TABLE 4:
RACE/ETHNICITY BY STATUS

	Couples	Single men	Single women	Male	Female
Non-Hispanic Whites (%)	70	11	12	2	5
Non-Hispanic African Americans (%)	49	14	15	4	18
Hispanics (%)	70	10	7	4	10
Other races and multiple races (%)	71	11	9	3	7

other race/ethnicity groups have 70 percent being in married couples among our population of non-dependent adults. By contrast, just 49 percent of African Americans are married; 18 percent are female-headed households with children, while another 29 percent are single men and women without children. Among the other race/ethnic groups, white adults are least likely to be a single adult with children and second most likely to be single without children. Among Hispanics, 14 percent are single adults with children, leaving just 17 percent being single adults without children.

Education

THERE ARE MANY REASONS FOR SUPPORTING increased educational attainment. For some, education plays a civilizing role for immigrants who don't know our language or customs. In a similar vein, education seems to encourage better behaviors and more personal satisfaction—higher rates of marriage, less smoking, healthier living, and more civic engagement. For others, especially businesses, better-educated workers are better workers. This has become more and more important as the production process has become more complex.

In today's world, education is used as the primary preparation for work, as those with more education are funneled into the highest-paying jobs. As Figure 1 shows, lifetime earnings rise with more education. While those with a high school diploma and no postsecondary education earn $1.3 million on average (or $32,500 a year over forty years), those with a bachelor's degree earn $2.3 million over a career, which is nearly $1 million more than those with just a high school education. Finally, those with a doctoral or professional degree average over $80,000 a year over forty years, leading to considerably more than $3 million over a career.

The United States' commitment to mass education has a long history. We were the first country to institute free and compulsory public elementary education in the late nineteenth century.

Before that, many schools required fees to be paid by the students or were run by churches. Other countries during this time period relied mainly on religious institutions and had widely varying levels of school-going among the young.

We expanded this commitment to mass attendance to high schools around the turn of the century. While relatively few completed high school, more and more children fourteen to sixteen years old attended school. The percentage of high school graduates expanded steadily throughout the first decades of the twentieth century. However, even with this steady improvement, just 30 percent of the workforce had a high school diploma in 1940, and a mere 12 percent had a bachelor's degree.

After the end of World War II, the American commitment to education increased with a push for all young people to finish high school with a degree and for a high proportion to pursue postsecondary

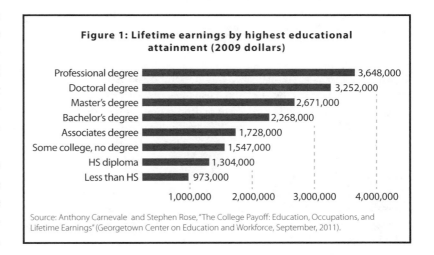

Figure 1: Lifetime earnings by highest educational attainment (2009 dollars)

Professional degree	3,648,000
Doctoral degree	3,252,000
Master's degree	2,671,000
Bachelor's degree	2,268,000
Associates degree	1,728,000
Some college, no degree	1,547,000
HS diploma	1,304,000
Less than HS	973,000

1,000,000 2,000,000 3,000,000 4,000,000

Source: Anthony Carnevale and Stephen Rose, "The College Payoff: Education, Occupations, and Lifetime Earnings" (Georgetown Center on Education and Workforce, September, 2011).

education. We implemented the GI Bill for returning veterans while we poured resources into educating the baby boom generation.

These commitments made the United States the undisputed leader in educational attainment and gave us a significantly higher rate of college completion than any other country. In the 1960s, when our lead in the share of the workforce with a college degree was large compared with most other industrialized countries, we continued to expand access to college, and eventually between 50 and 60 percent of each age cohort attended postsecondary institutions (with approximately 35 percent earning a degree). It should be noted that not all of this gain took place at four-year, bachelor's degree–granting institutions: in 1965, the fall enrollment in two-year schools was one million; by 1980, enrollment reached 4.3 million.

Since 1980, there has been hardly any expansion in the share of eighteen-year-olds enrolling in postsecondary education.[6] Yet, our competitors throughout the industrialized world have increased the college enrollment of their young people tremendously. Led by Finland, Canada, and South Korea, many countries have surpassed the United States in the percentage of twenty-five- to thirty-four-year-olds with a two- or four-year degree. Our fall to the middle of the pack of industrialized countries prompted President Barack Obama to call for new initiatives to dramatically increase college enrollment among young people.[7]

Nonetheless, Figure 2 shows a remarkable upgrading in educational attainment among work-

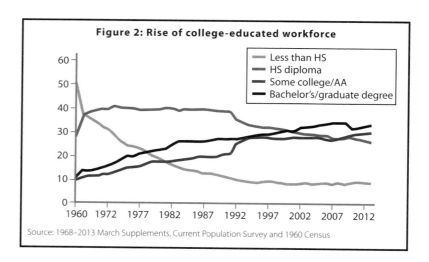

Figure 2: Rise of college-educated workforce

- Less than HS
- HS diploma
- Some college/AA
- Bachelor's/graduate degree

Source: 1968–2013 March Supplements, Current Population Survey and 1960 Census

ers over the period of this study (1960 to 2013). In 1960, over half of workers did not have a high school diploma. This share fell precipitously to under 10 percent by 1994 and has remained at this level since then (partially due to new immigrants with low education). By contrast, the share of those with a college education followed the opposite path and grew steadily. In 1960, only 21 percent of workers had attended college—10 percent with a BA or graduate degree and 11 percent with some college and perhaps an AA degree. By 2013, the college-going share had tripled to 64 percent—34 percent with a BA or graduate degree, 10 percent with a two-year degree, and 20 percent with an occupational/technical certificate or some college and no degree.

When the baby boomers first started finishing their education by going to college in record numbers, there were some indicators that perhaps we had gone too far and produced too many college graduates (see Richard Freeman's *The Overeducated American*). As we will show in the next chapter, this fear turned out to be unfounded as the earnings of workers with a BA relative to high-school-only workers skyrocketed.

Many view the rise in educational attainment as a simple reflection of an age of fast and accelerating technological change, particularly the rise

6. This stability is somewhat deceiving because it consists of offsetting trends. On the one hand, Hispanics and African Americans had much higher high school dropout rates than whites in 1980. Since then the share of these college-averse groups increased dramatically, which would decrease the overall share of each cohort that attends a postsecondary institution. However, over these same years, the share of Hispanics who failed to get a high school diploma or its equivalent decreased from 35 percent in 1980 to 18 percent in 2009, while the comparable rates for African Americans were 19 percent in 1980 and 9 percent in 2009.

7. In a 2011 piece in *The Undereducated American*, my co-author and I supported this call and showed how an extra twenty million college students through 2025 would increase economic output and decrease inequality.

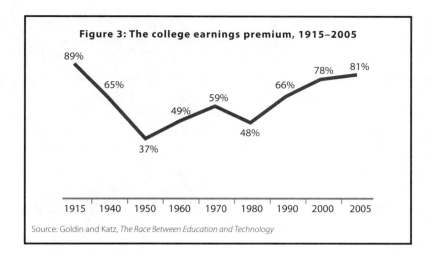

Figure 3: The college earnings premium, 1915–2005

89%

65%

49%

59%

37%

48%

66%

78%

81%

1915 1940 1950 1960 1970 1980 1990 2000 2005

Source: Goldin and Katz, *The Race Between Education and Technology*

of computers. This is a false view, as technological change has been persistent over the last two hundred years. The advent of the steam engine, internal combustion engine, telegraphy, telephones, air travel, and mass production of automobiles had at least as big an effect on their times as computerization has had on ours.

Historically, the education wage premium has risen and fallen depending on the complex interaction between supply and demand.[8] In *The Race Between Education and Technology*, Harvard economists Claudia Goldin and Lawrence Katz track the added earnings that college-educated workers have over those with just a high school education or less as the premium "skilled labor" receives to serve the needs of an ever more complicated production process.[9]

As Figure 3 shows, the college education premium started very high when very few people had attended postsecondary education. The Great Depression and World War II years (when there were wage and price controls) resulted in a large drop of the college premium. The curve shifts upward after 1950 as market forces play a bigger

role in driving the college premium back to its more typical levels. There is a blip in 1980 as the wave of young baby boomers entered the labor market, but this turned out to be a poor predictor for the future as the wage premium exploded after 1980.

Today, most parents and high school students appreciate the importance of postsecondary education and are focused on continuing schooling after high school. It is important to understand that the focus is not solely on the four-year degree. In papers I co-authored for the Georgetown Center on Education and the Workforce, data were presented on the advantages of technical and occupational certificates and two-year degrees. While a four-year degree works for many students, it is more difficult to attain and requires years of concerted effort. For many who have not had the best experiences in high school, it is important that there are alternative paths to prepare for adulthood and the labor market.

Despite the wide consensus that more education is almost always the best choice, there are a few voices that have arisen in the past several years that have challenged this consensus. Worries have arisen on three grounds:

1. the high cost of college has left many young adults with high student loan debts that have limited their choices and postponed major investments such as purchasing a home;
2. in today's tough economic times, many college graduates, especially recent graduates, can't find jobs that match their skills or pay anything like what previous college graduates made; and
3. the noncompletion rates are very high, meaning that many who start don't reach the finish line and aren't qualified for many high-paying jobs.

While all of these issues affect some people negatively, the advantages are still much greater. In February 2014, the Pew Research Center released

8. We would have liked to track the associate's/high school and bachelor's/associate's wage ratios, but information of those getting an associate's degree (as distinct from some college without a degree) only became available in the Current Population Survey in 1992, by which time most of the increase in earnings inequality had occurred.

9. The Belknap Press of Harvard University Press, Cambridge, Massachusetts: 2008.

a report entitled "The Rising Cost of Not Going to College," showing that among twenty-five- to thirty-two-year-olds the current advantages of earning a BA in terms of earnings, job satisfaction, and unemployment were much higher than in every year since 1965. As for the issue of getting a good job, 86 percent of Pew survey respondents say that they have a career-track job. My own research finds that 30 percent of recent college graduates (aged twenty-two to twenty-six) are currently in a job that doesn't utilize their talents and pays considerably less than typical BA jobs. These two findings aren't necessarily contradictory because many young people who are currently employed in a nonprofessional job expect to have one soon and hence give the positive answer on the Pew survey question.

The issues of costs and debts are complex and are often misrepresented in the mass media. Although there are schools that charge over $60,000 a year for tuition and fees, two out of three students enrolled there don't pay that amount but receive some sort of financial aid or tuition remittance. Consequently, the $100,000 debt stories are isolated cases: 35 percent graduate from a four-year school with no debt; of the remainder, the average debt is about $27,000; and 0.4 percent of students (1 in 250) graduate with $100,000 or more in debt. Finally, the overall default rate on student loans is under 10 percent (meaning that they haven't paid all of their loans), and the government fund that guarantees this debt has been running a small surplus every year over the last twenty.

In terms of graduation, the results are mixed and often driven by the poor preparation of students exiting high school. Of young people entering directly from high school and going to a four-year school, about two out of three will graduate within six years. Not surprisingly, those with good high school grades and high college entrance exams have higher rates, while those with lower scores have lower rates. If students take two or more years away from school before enrolling, their graduation rates fall by 20 to 30 percentage points.

Of those who originally enroll in two-year schools, only 40 percent earn a credential (AA, BA, or vocational/trade certificate) within six years.

This number is deceptive because a high proportion of their students are older and have been out of school many years, enroll part-time, or had low grades in high school. Of students with good grades who start at two-year schools, over 60 percent earn a credential within six years.

While these numbers aren't as high as one might hope, the end of earning a college degree should be a challenge that can only be reached with hard work and perseverance. What is clear is that those who succeed have a high probability of gaining tremendously from their experience.

Who Goes to College and Where Do They Go?

As will be shown below, having more education is strongly correlated with a greater likelihood of being married, getting a managerial or professional job, and having high family income. Given the importance of this decision, it is interesting to see the effects of family background on educational attainment.

Figure 4 shows that there is a remarkable difference in student achievement depending on family income (presented in quartiles—four groups from poorest 25 percent to richest 25 percent). Children from lower-income families tend to have less-educated parents. Studies show that these children have a significantly smaller vocabulary when they enter kindergarten. The cascading disadvantages of inferior elementary and high schools mean that they have lower academic abilities as they enter their final years in high school. For those in families in the bottom income quartile, nearly half score in the bottom test score quartile and only 10 percent score in the top test quartile.

The pattern is completely reversed for students from wealthy families in the top income quartile. A paltry 5 percent score in the bottom scoring quartile, while 48 percent score in the top quartile. Since scoring in the top quartile mostly leads to four-year colleges (and often the most selective four-year colleges), this discrepancy goes far in explaining why social mobility has declined in the United States over the past several decades. Although our "education-al meritocracy" appears to be a fair contest based on neutral standards, it is in fact a rigged game that favors children from high-income families. Consequently, it is not surprising that final educational outcomes are so different for children from different types of families. As Figure 5 shows, just 6 percent of students from high-income families do not attend college, while half of those from the lowest-income families do not attend college. Conversely, 60 percent of students from high-income families and 7 percent of students from low-income families get bachelor's degrees by age twenty-eight.

While these differing outcomes are driven primarily by differences in test scores, social class actually affects college attendance among students with similar scores. Figure 6 presents data on three groups: not surprisingly 80 percent of high-scoring rich kids go to four-year schools; by contrast, just over half of kids from low-income families go directly to four-year colleges (even though their likelihood of success is high), and 30 percent don't even go to college. These last numbers are very disappointing and lead to a waste of talent for the economy as a whole. Further, the fact that low-scoring students from high-income families go to college at almost the same rate as high-scoring low-income kids (although more start at two-year schools) shows the impact that expectations have on students of all classes.

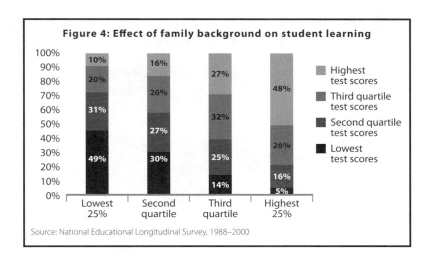

Figure 4: Effect of family background on student learning

Source: National Educational Longitudinal Survey, 1988–2000

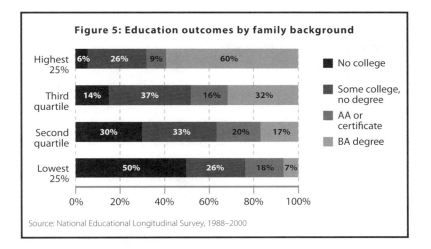

Figure 5: Education outcomes by family background

Source: National Educational Longitudinal Survey, 1988–2000

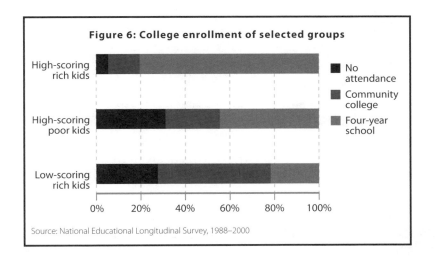

Figure 6: College enrollment of selected groups

Source: National Educational Longitudinal Survey, 1988–2000

DISTRIBUTION OF HOUSEHOLD STATUS BY EDUCATION LEVEL

	High school dropouts	HS diploma or GED	Some college or AA degree	BA degree	Graduate degree
Non-Hispanic whites (%)	6.6	29.1	28.6	22.7	13.0
Non-Hispanic African Americans (%)	13.4	33.0	31.6	13.6	8.4
Hispanics (%)	32.5	29.8	22.1	11.1	4.5
Asians, others, and multirace	8.2	20.2	23.2	28.1	20.4
All	11.0	29.1	27.7	20.6	11.8

The Populations with the Highest and Lowest Levels of Education

As Table 5 shows, there are large differences in attainment between Asians/others and whites versus African Americans and Hispanics (sometimes referred to as "underrepresented minorities"). Because so many Hispanics are recent migrants from Mexico and Central America, nearly one in three does not finish a high school diploma and only 15 percent have a BA or graduate degree. The children of immigrants and their children (third generation) have educational profiles closer to that of African Americans.

There are many stories in mass media about dropout rates of 50 percent in some inner-city high schools serving African Americans. This obscures the fact that African American children have made huge strides in closing the racial gap in high school graduation. Most people would not think that fewer than one in seven African Americans have failed to complete high school or earn an equivalency degree. The 22 percent share of African Americans with a BA or graduate degree still trails their white counterparts by 14 percentage points. The real outlier is the educational attainment of Asian and other races, with almost half having a BA or graduate degree.

Table 6 shows the distribution of household status by education level. Contrary to popular belief, it is not the case that highly educated people tend to lead more independent lives and marry less. In fact, there is a steep gradient from 62 percent of high school dropouts being married to 76 percent of those with a graduate degree being married. A higher marriage rate means that there are fewer highly educated adults living alone. In particular, the share of single women raising a family is at or near 10 percent for those with less than BA degree, and only 4 percent for those with a BA or graduate degree.

These patterns are based on people of similar educational backgrounds marrying each other. As Table 7 shows, over 50 percent of husbands who are high school dropouts are married to women who are high school dropouts as well. This meant that less than 20 percent of married men who were high school dropouts had wives who had attended any college, and only 4 percent had a BA or graduate degree. For married men who were high school graduates, half of their wives were high school graduates and 13 percent had a BA or graduate degree.

For highly educated married men, the patterns were reversed, as fully 75 percent of men with a graduate degree were married to women with at least a BA degree, with only 8 percent married to women who had not attended college. Married men with a BA were with women with advanced degrees 62 percent of time, and only in 14 percent of cases were they with someone who had not attended college.

TABLE 6:
MORE EDUCATED PEOPLE ARE MORE LIKELY TO BE MARRIED

	Couples	Single men	Single women	Single men with children	Single women with children
High school dropouts (%)	62	12	12	3	10
HS diploma or GED (%)	68	10	11	3	8
Some college or AA degree (%)	65	11	12	3	9
BA degree (%)	72	11	11	2	4
Graduate degree (%)	76	9	10	1	4

TABLE 7:
PEOPLE TEND TO MARRY PEOPLE WITH THE SAME LEVEL OF EDUCATION

	High school dropouts	HS diploma or GED	Some college or AA degree	BA degree	Graduate degree
HUSBAND'S EDUCATION					
High school dropouts (%)	51	31	14	3	1
HS diploma or GED (%)	9	51	26	10	3
Some college or AA degree (%)	3	25	45	19	8
BA degree	1	13	23	44	18
Graduate degree	1	7	16	35	40

The State of the Middle Class

THE TERM *MIDDLE CLASS* IS WIDELY USED—most Americans consider themselves part of it—but rarely defined. People usually reject the alternative categorizations—lower or upper class—because no one wants to be poor, and few consider themselves wealthy enough to be classified as rich.

Consider the following two families. In the first, the family income is $40,000: the husband works as a forklift operator at an assembly plant, while the wife stays at home caring for their two children. They own their home but have a mortgage of $150,000 on a home valued at $180,000. The other family is a suburban couple, a dentist and a psychologist, with a combined income of $250,000. Their house is worth $750,000 with a $300,000 outstanding mortgage. They own three cars; one child is in college, while another attends a local private school. Both families might describe themselves as being "strapped" for money, having little left over for frills. Both would probably consider themselves part of the middle class. At most, the first family might add the adjective "lower," the second "upper."

In other words, *middle class* has become a nearly all-inclusive category, one so broad that it not only blurs real distinctions in income, lifestyle, and well-being, but often clouds public discussion as well. For example, many cities have tried to attract the "middle class" into renovated downtown areas in order to bolster their tax bases. Unlike the outlying suburbs, though, these areas are not vacant; in order for one group to come in, another must leave.

The people who are displaced often consider themselves middle class, too, but they cannot afford to live in a neighborhood of increased rents, soaring property taxes, and fancy boutiques.

Another example is the effect of various federal tax reduction plans passed from 2001 through 2005. President George W. Bush promoted them as an overdue boon to the middle class, yet independent analysts have shown the dollar value is much greater for those with incomes above $150,000 than for families with incomes below $50,000. Clearly, both the families described above would have favored some tax relief for personal expenditures. This middle-class tax reform was worth $1,000 per year to families with a $40,000 income (on the basis of the child credit; without the child credit the tax deduction would have been just a couple of hundred dollars). By contrast, families with incomes over $250,000 had a tax reduction that could exceed $25,000, while a family at the $250,000 level paid $10,000 less.

This confusion surrounding the term *middle class* shows that we must take special care in defining terms and distinguishing various groups within the population in order to have informed debate about pressing social issues. Data on the poster and in the graphs and tables in this book reveal the significant presence of many different social and ethnic groups in the $40,000–$100,000 income range. This income group includes approximately the same number of high school–educated, blue-collar households as professional-managerial households with college degrees; it also comprises clerical and sales workers as well as people of all ages, including retired people and members of minority groups. The existence of this large, relatively heterogeneous group is cited as proof that Americans are basically all part of the same social group, the middle class, with relative unity of interests.

However, it is no guarantee of social equality. For high school–educated, blue-collar families, blacks, and Latinos, $100,000 represents nearly the top of their earning potential. For college-educated professionals and managers, on the other hand, $100,000 is just below their median. College-educated workers with incomes in the $40,000–100,000 range are often at the beginning of their careers. So, for many members of the "middle class," $100,000 represents the most they can aspire to; for others, it is a stepping-stone on the way to a higher standard of living.

Incomes

INCOME IS USUALLY REGARDED AS A PROXY FOR one's standard of living and perhaps well-being. Obviously, this does not mean that everyone with a low income is unhappy and everyone with a high income is content. Rather, most people believe that access to more and better goods, houses, and amenities makes life more enjoyable. Higher incomes, then, are preferable and can serve as an indicator of "leading the good life."

Family size presents another problem in relating income to well-being. For example, who is better off: an individual with an income of $25,000 or a family of three with $50,000? This problem affects our ability to make historical comparisons, because family sizes have declined. An inflation-adjusted income of $50,000 in 1970 was likely to have supported four people, but today it might cover only three people.

At first glance, it seems that the solution to this would be simply to divide income by the number of people in the family. However, this approach does not account for "economies of scale"—costs don't go up in proportion to the number of individuals in the household because they can share expenses. The old phrase "two can live as cheaply as one" is an exaggeration, but providing for two does not cost twice as much. A number of approaches have been proposed to account for this. These are known as equivalency scales of need to income for different household sizes and are used in setting the poverty income cutoffs for families of different size. Most adjustments find that it requires twice as much for a family of four to live at the same level

as a single person. Thus, $25,000 for a single person is equivalent to $50,000 for a family of four. If there were no economies of scale, then the family of four with $50,000 would equal $12,500 for a single person.

Another factor that affects how people feel about their income is how it compares with that of their peers. For those who live in a suburban neighborhood where most family incomes are over $100,000, then an income of $50,000 will seem low. However, in an inner-city neighborhood with an average family income of $20,000, this same $50,000 will seem quite high. An income of $40,000 might support a comfortable standard of living in smaller cities and rural areas but wouldn't go as far in many large cities, where rents and housing costs are high. But there are other trade-offs that make simple comparisons difficult—for example, wide-open spaces and recreational opportunities in the countryside versus the cultural opportunities and excitement of big cities. Finally, students and other young people have a different problem in analyzing these income figures. Because they have had little experience running households themselves, they are unaware of all the expenses involved and tend to think that money goes farther than it does.

To put some context into what various incomes mean, a series of benchmarks are presented in the accompanying sidebar. There is a long discussion of whether the poverty line is too high or too low followed by definitions of low, medium, and high family budgets. This dividing line will be used later

Defining 2014 Standards of Living for a Family of Three

The Poverty Line ($19,090) Between 1963 and 1965, Mollie Orshansky—an economist working for the Social Security Administration—developed an approach for determining the poverty threshold for different-sized families. She built her analysis around the Department of Agriculture's finding that families were spending about one-third of their after-tax income on food. At that same time, the Department of Agriculture produced a series of four nutritionally adequate food consumption baskets. The "economy food plan" was the least expensive and became the basis of the poverty line (after being multiplied by three).

For only a few years annual updates in the poverty line were determined by changes in the cost of the economy food plan. But this approach was dropped in 1969 as the share of food of family budgets dropped below a third. In its stead, the poverty line was adjusted each year to account for changes in the overall inflation rate as reported by the Bureau of Labor Statistics. Each year, the Department of Health and Human Services publishes in the Federal Register the updated thresholds (see https://www.federal register.gov/articles/2014/01/22/2014-01303/ annual-update-of-the-hhs-poverty-guidelines).

There are many critics of this approach. On the left, many commentators have felt that the food approach was always questionable and under-estimated the costs of a minimally adequate standard of living. Further, poor people are not nutritional experts with access to the best food buys (studies have shown that poor areas have higher-than-average food prices).

Finally, another group of analysts believes that the number of poor people is underestimated because, they argue, poverty is not simply some inflation-adjusted standard. They would define poverty relative to the standard of living in the country at that time—for example, setting the poverty line at 50 percent of median family income.[9] Doing this would raise the income cutoff for poverty for a family of three to about $30,000 and increase the number of officially classified poor people by three-quarters from 15 to almost 25 percent of the population.

On the other side of the spectrum, conservatives argue that the poverty threshold is set too high because the value of food stamps and Medicaid are not included. The Reagan administration attempted to have these noncash benefits counted as income, which would have reduced the number of people in poverty by one-third with the stroke of a pen. Congressional resistance blocked this revision because of the fear that an officially lower estimate of the poor population would have led to a perception that we had solved our poverty problem. Unfortunately, as will be discussed later, the conditions of the bottom fifth of the income ladder have not improved over the last twenty years (as is particularly evident in the rising number of homeless people).

As this brief discussion demonstrates, defining poverty is very politically charged because movements in the poverty rate are used to reflect the state of our economy. These disputes make it very unlikely that government officials will change the current approach beyond adjusting the current poverty line for inflation.

Low Budget ($33,408) The family in this category most likely lives in rental housing without air-conditioning. It performs many necessary maintenance tasks, repairs, and similar services

9. James Smith proposes a middle ground—setting the poverty level at its 1963 level and then raising it by the rate of inflation and one-half the real per capita growth rate.

(Continued)

for itself and makes use of free public recreational facilities. Compared with those in higher budget levels, this family eats less meat and more potatoes and drinks less wine and liquor but more beer. According to the Bureau of Labor Statistics (BLS), the low budget "is not designed as a subsistence budget" and should enable the family to maintain "a sense of self-respect and social participation."

Medium Budget ($57,270) The medium budget is supposed to provide a higher standard of living. This family probably owns its own home but has fifteen years left on the mortgage. Instead of having new appliances and cars, this family rotates through used cars and has cheap-

er or older versions of cell phones, HDTVs, game consoles, and other modern conveniences. This family tends to take vacations close to home and may save on accommodations by staying with relatives or camping out.

High Budget ($81,113) The families at this level and above own their own home and have a new automobile and a more complete line of household appliances and computerized gadgets. It can pay for rather than perform many necessary services, and it takes vacations to other places in the United States and abroad. This income represents the minimum necessary to support a "suburban, upper-middle-class" lifestyle.

in showing the changing size of the middle class—defined as those with incomes between the low and high budget lines.

The definitions of the budgets in the accompanying sidebar assume a family of three and are based on multiples of the government's poverty thresholds. By contrast, income figures are reported as gross amounts (that is, before taxes are deducted) and include earnings (salaries and wages), returns on investment (dividends, rents, and royalties), and cash payments from government (Social Security, retirement benefits, welfare, and unemployment compensation). The incomes of husbands and wives are added together along with any earnings from other family members (for example, working children) to form a combined family income. The following sources, however, are excluded from the government's definition of income: the value of employer-provided benefits (for example, medical insurance and pension contributions), noncash government benefits (for example, food stamps, Medicare), and capital gains from the sale of long-held assets.

Ideally, the best measure of standard of living is one that encompasses many years and adjusts for

changes in living conditions. For example, people who are going to graduate school often have very low incomes and might even be classified as being poor. But this is a temporary condition and this person's long-term prospects are much better than their current state.

In fact, there is a fair amount of year-to-year variation associated with periodic good and bad events. Of those that are in the bottom 20 percent of the income ladder, one-third will have large income gains (averaging 80 percent) and will jump up many rungs. Similarly, one-third in the top 20 percent will drop out because of isolated good years. This churn at the top means that, although one in six are in households that have yearly incomes above $100,000, six in ten will have incomes over $100,000 at least once over ten years.

So the poster is a snapshot in time. People, however, have longer time horizons, thinking both about their past and about what their future will hold. The information on the poster is comprehensive but represents only the beginning of a discussion about living conditions in the United States.

Changes over Time

As was mentioned above, the original poster was meant to show the high level of inequality at the time. Today it is more unequal. As Figure 7 shows, there was very little real income gain in the bottom third of the income ladder. Starting at the median, the 2012 line gets farther and farther away from the 1979 line, indicating larger and larger gains over these 33 years.

Another way to look at this relationship is to show the rate of change at each percentile level in 1979 and 2012. Figure 8 shows close to zero growth through incomes up to $30,000. After rising to 10 percent at the median, the rate of growth moves steadily higher up to 44 percent at the 95th percentile. The gain of the 99th percentile dwarfs all other gains. On the poster, there are 882 icons on the big format income line that ends at incomes of $150,000. Of the 118 icons with incomes above $150,000, 62 fall into the range between $150–200,000; another 38 are between $200–300,000, leaving 9 icons between $300–400,000 and 9 above $400,000. The minimum value for the top couple (who represent the two-tenths of one percent of the income ladder is just under $1 million.

It is this unusual gain at the top that is the basis of Occupy Wall Street's slogan, "we are the 99 percent." The $100 million golden parachutes of corporate executives (even the number two executive at Yahoo! got one of these in 2014 after serving just fifteen months) who are let go because of subpar performances certainly seem an indication that something is wrong. Yet no one knows how to stop this.

In the early 1960s, President Kennedy used public shaming of large pay packages to corporate executives to reverse these decisions. That obviously is not a viable option today, and Congress has

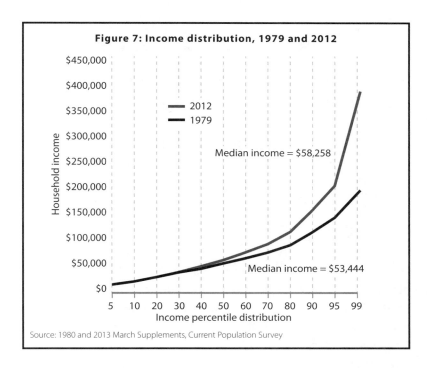

Figure 7: Income distribution, 1979 and 2012

Source: 1980 and 2013 March Supplements, Current Population Survey

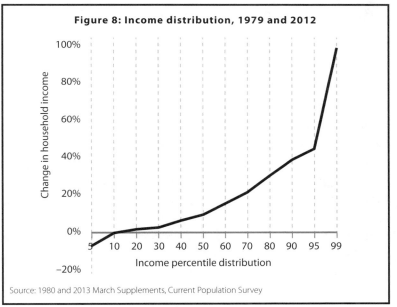

Figure 8: Income distribution, 1979 and 2012

Source: 1980 and 2013 March Supplements, Current Population Survey

not been able to come up with new legislation to prohibit this practice. The easiest way to respond would be to have new tax brackets that kick in at incomes of $1 million and $10 million a year, but this is anathema for most Republicans and some Democrats.

Even the public is ambivalent when it comes to high tax brackets. For example, opinion polls show that over 60 percent of the public is against inheritance taxes even if the tax only begins on

TABLE 8:
SHRINKING MIDDLE CLASS, BUT MORE ARE WELL-OFF

	1979 (%)	2014 (%)	Change
Poor	9.8	10.5	+ 0.7
Near poor	14.2	12.8	- 1.4
Middle class	47	36.5	- 10.5
Well-off	29	40.3	+ 11.3

estates over $3 million. There is a sense that people "earned" their money even if they have great wealth—e.g., entertainers, athletes, or famous entrepreneurs such as Bill Gates, Mark Zuckerberg, and Michael Dell.

Furthermore, many people think that the government spends too much, a notion stoked by decades of conservative invective. One of the biggest oddities of American politics is that the states with the biggest conservative vote are the ones that get the best deal from the federal government's taxation and spending policies. Studies that look at the net balance between all money sent to the federal government versus all federal dollars to state individuals, companies, and governments find that the states of the Southwest, South, and Mountain regions are net gainers, while the states of the Northeast and Pacific Coast are net payers.

In the 2012, the ten states that had the worst negative balance with the federal government—paying more taxes than benefits received—all went for Obama, while eight of the ten states with the largest positive balance went for his Republican challenger, Mitt Romney. The antigovernment populations of the net benefactors aren't against all government programs. In fact, they like agricultural subsidies, defense spending, and Social Security. For them, these programs are appropriate, while the government programs for the nondeserving poor in urban states should be cut.

Using the income cutoffs described by our benchmarks, Table 8 shows the change from 1979 to 2014 for four groups—poor, near poor, middle class, and well-off. Because of the deep recession

from which we haven't fully recovered, the share of the poster's nondependent adults in poverty rose modestly from 9.8 percent in 1979 to 10.5 percent in 2014 (it had been 9.3 percent in 2007, the year of the previous edition of the poster). The next group—the near poor—declined by over one percentage point, meaning that the share of this population in households below middle-class living standards decreased from 1979 to 2014.

But what is most striking about Table 8 is that the share of adults in the middle class plummeted by over 10 percent. However, this is good news in that this "shrinking of the middle class" was entirely due to the growing share of those with "well-off" incomes. Given that the economy has expanded by 60 percent per person in real terms, a much bigger pie, even if it is divided unequally, will mean some economic growth for most households. Since our benchmarks are based on absolute living standards that only change with inflation, any growth that is captured by those with middle-class incomes means that the distribution shifts upward.

This approach has two failings—one suggesting a more optimistic conclusion, the other a less optimistic one. On the one hand, spending on health care has been one of the biggest gainers and has led to longer life expectancies and healthier lives in old age (despite our worsening diet and higher levels of diabetes). Most people's spending in this area is subsidized by employers, who pay approximately 70 percent of insurance costs, and by the government through clinics, Medicaid, and Medicare. From an economist's point of view, this represents personal consumption that is not included in the

DISTRIBUTION OF INCOME BY HOUSEHOLD STATUS

	Married (%)	Single men (%)	Single women (%)	Single men with children (%)	Single women with children (%)	All (%)	Number of icons on poster
HOUSEHOLD INCOMES (THOUSANDS OF DOLLARS)							
0–20	7	34	43	17	30	16	157
20–40	15	28	28	27	28	19	194
40–60	16	17	14	20	17	16	158
60–80	15	9	7	13	10	13	130
80–100	12	4	3	8	6	10	98
100–125	12	3	2	6	3	9	89
125–150	7	2	1	3	2	6	56
>150	16	3	1	6	3	12	118
All	100	100	100	100	100	100	1000

monetary income figures reported in Table 8 and hence underestimates the gains in living standards.

On the other hand, people's desires are affected by the cultural norms of the day. If lots of people have cell phones, computers, and HDTVs, this becomes a standard that everyone feels that they must meet. Furthermore, our economy is built around the auto, without which it is very difficult to live. So Table 8 (showing income gains at the middle) isn't inconsistent with Figure 8 (showing much more income gains for those in the top quarter of the income distribution); they just tell two different stories—increasing living standards and increasing inequality.

The Income Distributions of the Different Populations on the Poster

Table 9 presents the distribution of income for the five household types. As is evident, the share of married couples in the lowest income level (up to $20,000, which is less than the poverty income for a family of four) is just 7 percent, a level much lower than the other household types. By contrast, fully 43 percent of single women are in the lowest income tier, with many of them being elderly retirees whose husbands have died. It should be noted that this does not mean that they are officially categorized as being poor since the income cutoff for poverty for a single person over sixty-five years old was just $11,000 in 2012. With the exception of single male–headed families with 17 percent in the lowest income category, single male and female-headed households had at least 30 percent with low incomes.

As noted above, standard of living differs by the number of the people in the household, which strongly affects how we consider single-adult households. A way to rectify this is to adjust income for number of members present and report incomes as "family of three equivalents." Using this approach, only 113 icons, rather than 157, would have incomes below $20,000 (which is close to the poverty line of $19,090 for a family of three). The incidence of family households (married couples and single adults with children) in the lowest income category remains the same. But there is

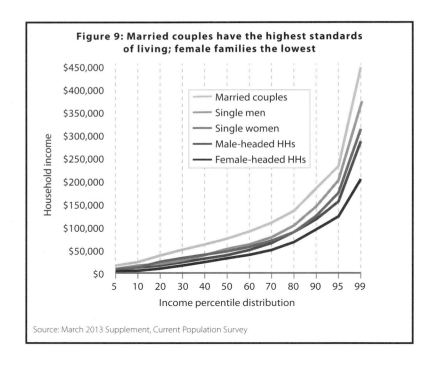

Figure 9: Married couples have the highest standards of living; female families the lowest

Source: March 2013 Supplement, Current Population Survey

lents) for the five types of households. Married couples have the highest incomes by a substantial amount because they often have multiple incomes and because more stable people are married and tend to have higher earnings. Using size-adjusted incomes, the second-highest income group is single men because they usually have higher earnings than single women. Although single-male family householders made as much as single men, they have to support more people and therefore their income profile is similar to that of single women. Finally, female-headed households have lower earnings and more people to support and hence trail the other household types.

a big effect on single people as the share of these households with equivalent incomes of $20,000 or less drops to 18 percent for men and 22 percent for women.

Figure 9 presents the income distribution based on size-adjusted incomes (family of three equiva-

Turning to education, Table 10 shows the joint distribution of education and income by the number of icons on the poster. It is immediately evident that virtually all of those who didn't finish high school are clustered in incomes below $60,000. Of the 290 icons representing those with a high school

TABLE 10:
EDUCATION BY INCOME, BY ICONS ON POSTER

HOUSEHOLD INCOMES (THOUSANDS OF DOLLARS)	High school dropouts	HS diploma or GED	Some college or AA degree	BA degree	Graduate degree	All education levels
$0–20	40	55	41	15	6	157
$20–40	34	72	54	25	9	194
$40–60	17	54	48	27	12	158
$60–80	9	41	41	26	13	130
$80–100	4	26	30	25	13	98
$100–125	3	20	26	26	14	89
$125–150	1	10	15	18	12	56
Greater than $150	1	12	22	44	39	118
ALL INCOMES	109	290	277	206	118	1000

education, 181 are in households with incomes below $60,000 and just 42 have incomes above $100,000. By contrast, over the half of icons representing those with a graduate degree (65 out of 118) have incomes over $100,000, with only 27 icons for this most educated groups in households with incomes below $60,000. While the middle education category (some college plus those with a two-year degree) has a distribution similar to the entire population, those with BAs are more concentrated in the higher-income categories: 88 of 206 icons are located above $100,000 and just 67 are below $60,000.

Figure 10 provides an alternative angle on income distribution by educational attainment: as education rises, each of the income lines on this figure moves higher. Because this figure has to have a top value, the differences at the lower levels are not as dramatic as the differences in the actual values. In terms of medians, those who haven't finished high school have a median household income of $30,600; those who graduated from high school but never attend postsecondary institutions have a median of $52,900; the median of those with some college or an AA degree is $64,900; for those with BAs it is $96,500, and for those with a graduate degree it is $122,500.

Finally, this distribution can be presented as the share of each education at the different income levels (Figure 11). The different waves of colors show visually that most of the lower income levels are dominated by those with lower levels of education. The relatively few BA and graduate degree holders are mostly younger and may even still be in school but not living with their parents. Conversely, the small bands of lower-educated workers with the highest incomes show that there is some room for those who have built their own successful business even without earning a BA degree.

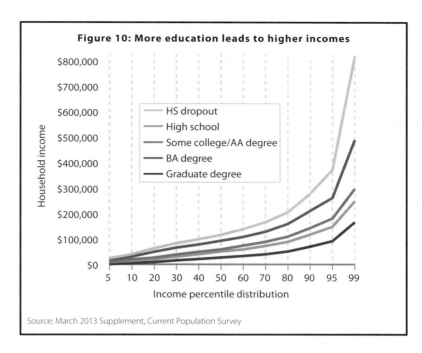

Figure 10: More education leads to higher incomes

Source: March 2013 Supplement, Current Population Survey

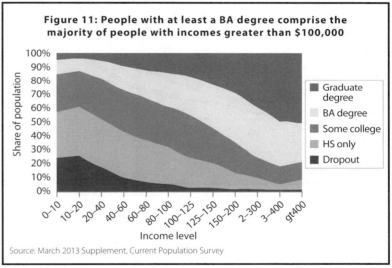

Figure 11: People with at least a BA degree comprise the majority of people with incomes greater than $100,000

Source: March 2013 Supplement, Current Population Survey

Figure 12 shows income distribution by race/ethnicity. As is immediately obvious, non-Hispanic whites, Asians, and other races have higher incomes than African Americans and Hispanics (sometimes referred to as "underrepresented minorities") by about 40 percent throughout the whole distribution. The growth and success of Asians, the dominant group in the "other" category, has been very impressive. While some come to this country with advanced degrees (especially those from India), there are many cases of the children of Asian immigrants translating educational achievement into labor market success. In terms of medians, the high-income groups are at $75,000, while African Americans are at $47,000 and Hispanics at $43,000.

Although great disparities remain between African Americans and whites, there have been many improvements over the last sixty-five years (most data on Hispanics don't go back this far). In 1950, one-half of employed black women were domestics and one-half of black men were laborers; over 90

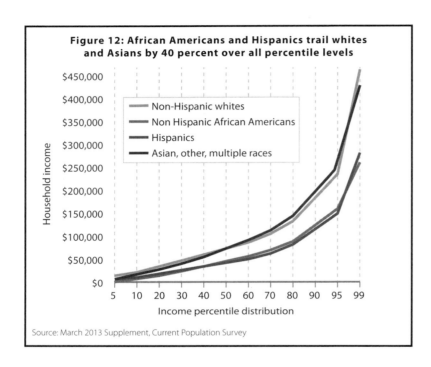

Figure 12: African Americans and Hispanics trail whites and Asians by 40 percent over all percentile levels

Source: March 2013 Supplement, Current Population Survey

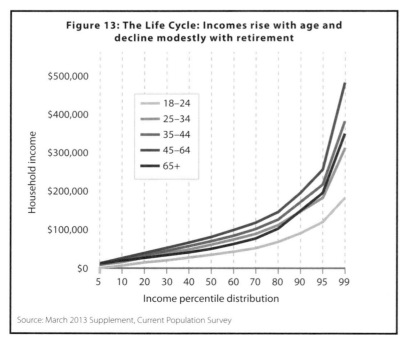

Figure 13: The Life Cycle: Incomes rise with age and decline modestly with retirement

Source: March 2013 Supplement, Current Population Survey

percent had not finished high school. At the same time, there were legally segregated public facilities, and the public use of derogatory language toward minorities was common. Clearly, much has changed as African Americans have narrowed the education gap with whites tremendously, and a growing number of African Americans belong to the professional and managerial ranks, a movement that has been led by public-sector hiring. On the other hand, much remains to be done before full integration is achieved. Blacks and Latinos suffer disproportionately from poor living conditions, low-paying employment with frequent intervals of unemployment, and a troubled public school system.

The final income chart shows the differences by age, reflecting a clear life-cycle pattern—start with low income when starting out, improve steadily through ages fifty to fifty-five, then slowly decline, especially after retirement, which occurs at varying ages after sixty. Another factor that affects living standards is the presence of children. Since these income figures are family of three equivalents, adding a child increases the number of people that have to be supported and decreases living standards. Similarly, when children leave home to set off on their own, this reduces the number of people in the household and increases living standards.

As Figure 13 shows, the lowest incomes are for those aged eighteen to twenty-four who are no longer living with their parents (median income of $36,700). As people age into their late twenties and early thirties, they start to find the appropriate niche median income rises to $62,300. By the late thirties, workers are in their prime earning years (median income of thirty-five- to forty-four-year-olds is $70,900). After age forty-five and before retirement, median income rises to $81,600, as earnings rise a bit for some and children move out of the house, reducing family size and the number of people dividing the income.

Finally, adults over sixty-five have a sharp reduction in cash income (with a median income of $51,400). Yet, in annual surveys from the Employee Benefits and Retirement Institute, almost two-thirds of retired people report living as well as they did in their fifties. This is due to a number of factors: lower expenses because mortgages are often paid off; self-sufficient middle-aged children; no commuting and working expenses; the benefits of more free time; and diminished expectations, in that people adjust to their circumstances. It should also be noted that medical expenses are very high, and Medicare is a valuable insurance program that isn't included as part of their cash income.

Going forward, there is some concern that tomorrow's retirees won't have it as good as today's retirees because of the decline in company pensions. Pensions have been replaced by individual 401(k) and related plans. These plans are actually better than company pensions for people who change jobs often, because pensions are based on years of service and highest pay; without a lot of years of service, the cash flow in retirement will be quite low. But individual retirement accounts shift the investment risk to workers and also can be reduced when people take out loans during tough times.

So it is a bit uncertain how the large waves of baby boomers, who are retiring at a rate of ten thousand a day for the next fifteen years, will fare. One trend has already started—retiring later. For many professionals, this is a choice to keep engaged as many wonder what they will do once they stop working. For others, this is more of a necessity to postpone using their retirement savings for later years. In the end, the inequality that exists among the working is replicated among the elderly.

One final issue that needs to be addressed in discussing family well-being is that of volatility. Virtually all of the data on socioeconomic conditions are like the poster, in that they are snapshots of a specific point in time. When comparing different periods, the changing experiences of individuals aren't used; instead, researchers align "similarly situated" people—i.e., the median in one year versus the median in another year. The experiences of individuals are much more difficult to know and are limited to "longitudinal panel surveys" that follow the same people year in and year out.[10]

In studies using the Panel Study on Income Dynamics (the longest-running longitudinal survey), I find a tremendous amount of yearly volatility: approximately one-third of those who are in the bottom or top twenty of the population are there for one isolated year and "revert" toward their normal position that is more in the middle of the income ladder. This means that over half of adults experience at least one year with incomes over $100,000 or incomes under $35,000.

By and large, incomes tend to rise over time, for one-third of the population actually has lower inflation-adjusted incomes today than they had ten years earlier. This means that even if we understand the gross movements of incomes, the unevenness of individuals' experiences adds an element that shouldn't be neglected.

10. Social Security and IRS administrative records can also provide multiyear data, but except in isolated cases, this information is not available to all researchers.

Wealth

WEALTH IS DIFFERENT FROM INCOME. *Income* is the amount of money that comes into a household from varying sources during the course of a year. *Wealth* (sometimes referred to as net worth), on the other hand, is the total monetary value of what a household owns, minus debts. This includes consumer durables such as houses, cars, stereos, the value of owned businesses, and so on, plus financial assets such as stocks, bonds, savings accounts, property, cash value of life insurance policies, and the like. The majority of most Americans' wealth is the equity value of their homes. Business assets are another source for many people.

By contrast, a quarter of American households only have at most $1,400 in their checking and/or savings accounts. Another quarter has very little financial wealth as the median household level of financial wealth is just $17,000.[11] And the situation isn't that much better for those nearing or starting retirement: the 25th-percentile value is just $3,200 and the median value is $40,000.

So who is rich? Once we realize that there are two measures, this question becomes a bit more complicated. Consider two households: a retirement-age couple with a net worth of $2 million ($1 million in equity in their home) and an income of $65,000 ($35,000 in dividends and interest and $30,000 in Social Security checks); or a young dual-profession couple in their midthirties with

11. The data on wealth and income presented here come from the 2010 Survey of Consumer Finances conducted every three years by the Federal Reserve Board.

one child, an income of $240,000 a year, and a net worth of $160,000 ($100,000 in home equity and just $60,000 of retirement and savings accounts). The first couple is at the 96th percentile of the wealth distribution and 65th percentile of the income distribution, while the second couple is at the 96th percentile of the income distribution and the 65th percentile of the wealth distribution.

The easy answer is that they are both well-off. The older couple has much more wealth and sizable annual income (above the median), while the younger couple has lots of income but a relatively modest amount of wealth. The older couple has fewer expenses because they have no mortgage to pay off, have a full complement of consumer goods, and their children are now adults. The younger couple has a child to send to college and a big mortgage, but this couple has many years to earn more and accumulate much more wealth. So these two couples are at different points in their life cycle and at different points on the income and wealth distributions.

Table 11 presents data on income wealth by level of income based on groups from lowest to highest income. The first four groups are ordered groups of 20 percent each. Thus, the first quintile represents the holdings of the poorest 20 percent of the population followed by next three quintiles. From the 80th percentile and above, there are a series of finer gradations of people with high incomes until the highest category represents those with incomes over $1.5 million (the top two-tenths of 1 percent).

TABLE 11:
INCOME AND WEALTH HOLDINGS BY INCOME LEVEL

	Average wealth	Share of total wealth (%)	Number of dollar signs on poster
HOUSEHOLD INCOME LEVEL			
Bottom 20 percent	115,993	5	1
Second quintile	130,884	5	1.5
Third quintile	198,686	8	2
Fourth quintile	294,551	12	3
80th to 90th percentiles	560,598	11	5.6
90th to 95th percentiles	1,067,037	11	11
95th to 99th percentiles	2,985,831	24	30
99th to 99.8th percentiles	8,274,258	13	83
Top two-tenths of 1 percent	25,142,427	10	251

The three columns on this table represent average wealth of the group (e.g., the top tenths of one percent average over $25.1 million), the share of total wealth held by that group, and the share of total income of the group. While the first column of numbers is the basis of the wealth dollar signs on the poster, the last two columns show the shares of wealth and income based on income categories are not that radically different. For example, the richest 1 percent by income (incomes greater than $615,000) has 23 percent of all wealth and 17 percent of all income.[12]

As our two-family comparison showed, there are a number of reasons that wealth and income aren't as correlated as many people would think. Retired people, for example, tend to have low incomes but high accumulated wealth; farmers are another group that fits this mold. On the other hand, wealth is mainly accumulated after the age of forty. Therefore, there are many young professionals who have high incomes but have yet to build up many assets; in fact, they are likely to have

12. Because these data on based on the finance survey while the poster is based on the March supplement of the CPS, the cutoff for the top 1 percent is different in the two surveys.

high debts because of student loans and their initial purchase of a home.

Finally, 5 percent of the wealth and 3 percent of the income is held by people in households with incomes below $20,340. The modest wealth holding of this group represents elderly households with very low incomes but fair amounts of wealth in terms of the value of their homes and even sometimes investment and savings accounts. The less-than-perfect alignment of wealth and income means that the top 5 percent of income households have 47 percent of the wealth and 34 percent of the income. By contrast, the bottom 60 percent of the population (those with incomes below $58,000) has 18 percent of the wealth and 23 percent of the income.

Table 12 presents data on the distribution of wealth on the basis of wealth (going back to our two families, the retired couple was at the 65th percentile of income but the 96th percentile of wealth—it is this second distribution that we are now looking at). Now, the distribution of wealth is much more unequally distributed than income, as the bottom 60 percent only holds 4 percent of the wealth, while the wealthiest 5 percent has 60

TABLE 12:
WEALTH CONCENTRATION BY WEALTH LEVEL

	Average wealth ($)	Share of total wealth ($)
HOUSEHOLD WEALTH LEVEL		
Lowest quintile	-15,711	-1
Second quintile	23,344	1
Third quintile	98,439	3
Fourth quintile	285,527	10
80th to 90th percentiles	711,430	13
90th to 95th percentiles	1,515,377	13
95th to 99th percentiles	3,821,354	27
99th to 99.8th percentiles	11,959,683	17
Top two-tenths of 1 percent	46,669,033	16

percent. The top two-tenths of 1 percent has a net minimum wealth holding of $19 million, and the average for the group is just under $47 million. This group has more wealth than the bottom 80 percent of wealth holders combined, even though there are four hundred people in the bottom group for every person in the top group.

By contrast, virtually no one in the bottom 20 percent of the wealth distribution has a positive net worth. Because so many people have levels of debt significantly greater than their assets, the average wealth for this group is a negative $15,711. The average wealth of the third quintile of wealth holders has less wealth then the average of the bottom quintile based on income (once again a sign of the less-than-full connection of wealth and income).

The distribution is even more skewed when people's houses, cars, and consumer durables are excluded. In terms of all financial assets, the bottom 60 percent of the population has just 2 percent of all financial assets, while the top 5 percent have 65 percent of the total.

Finally there is the issue of debt, which has become a very charged subject with many misconceptions. One quarter of households have no debt.

Surprisingly, low-income households are more likely to have no debt than middle- and upper-income households: 47 percent of the lowest income quintile and 33 percent of the second quintile have no debt. When these low-income households have debt, it is likely to cause more disruptions, but many low-income people suffer from easy access to credit. Some of the worst abuses involve payday loan companies, which end up charging people astronomically high interest rates for short-term loans.

In another surprise, 60 percent of households pay their credit card bills on time and have no outstanding credit card debt. For the past many years, those without credit card debt stood at 54 percent, so it appears that the crisis of 2008 and its aftermath have led more people to be wary of running up debt. According to the 2010 Survey of Consumer Finances, 28 percent of households have outstanding credit card balances of $1,000 or more; 14 percent have $5,000 or more; and just 9 percent have balances greater than $10,000. These numbers contrast sharply with the number—$15,000 as the average of credit card debt—that is cited by some using an inappropriate data source from the Federal Reserve Board.

Finally, 82 percent of household debt is based on residential property. Historically, this has been considered a safe form of debt because it was backed by an asset that could be easily sold to pay off the outstanding balance on the loan. In the past, larger down payments were required (usually at least 20 percent of the purchase price), and this created a cushion in the event of a temporary downturn in housing prices. And most downturns were temporary and not severe.

This changed in the 2000s as the financial industry discovered that they could make lots of money packaging mortgages into mortgage bonds and selling them to high-end investors and institutional buyers. The credit-rating agencies went along with this strategy and pleased their clients by giving AAA ratings to these bonds. Furthermore, mortgages to high-risk borrowers were particularly attractive because they carried higher interest payments and could lead to big profit margins.[13]

A toxic feedback loop developed as regulators, journalists, and financial experts minimized the downside risk. Instead, the drive for profits and commissions drove up housing prices as more and more buyers were being approved for loans, often with fraudulent documentation. The old standards were dropped, and speculators pounced, buying and selling properties to "flip" quickly for instant profits.

13. See the first two chapters of my book *Rebound* for a full discussion of these events.

A few brave souls spoke up—and were ignored. Then in 2008, a financial edifice that was based on low rates of loan failures imploded. For a while, most of the twenty-five largest financial institutions were technically insolvent and should have been closed. Fearing a total collapse of the economy, the federal government and Federal Reserve stepped in with a huge bailout package that eventually stabilized the situation.

Unemployment shot up to over 10 percent, and home prices plummeted by 20 to 50 percent. In a period of months, millions of households were unable to pay their mortgages and additional millions were "underwater" (owing more than their equity). Some people got in trouble because they used their home "like an ATM," converting some of their home equity to cash for home upgrades or other purposes. In 2010, of the two-thirds of homeowners that had mortgages, 17 percent had refinanced and extracted equity, 16 percent had a home equity loan, and 9 percent had a second mortgage.

In the "dull" past, people got a mortgage and paid it off as they aged. For many, this meant hosting end-of-mortgage parties when the loan was paid off. In 1989, only 6 percent of homeowners over seventy-five still had a balance due on their mortgages; among sixty-five- to seventy-four-year-olds, this figure was 21 percent. By contrast, in 2010 the comparable figures were 21 percent and 37 percent.

Occupations

IN PREVIOUS EDITIONS OF THE POSTER, THE colors on the icons represented occupations or employment status if not in the labor force. The first thing that should be noted is that there are a lot of nonworkers. For the population as a whole, just a tad less than half are employed and create the value to support the entire population. If we just look at those sixteen and older, 41 percent don't work because they are retired, unemployed, keeping house (the census term for a housewife), or out of the labor force (on welfare, disabled, or homeless). And if we limit the analysis to the nondependent adults represented on the poster, 20 percent are retired and 38 percent aren't working. Not surprisingly, women are more likely than men to not be working: 44 percent of the female icons and 31 percent of the male icons on the poster aren't working, with only 4 percentage points of this 13-point difference due to more female retirees.

The six occupational categories are hierarchically ordered: (1) managers/doctors/lawyers; (2) professionals in business, education, and health care; (3) clerical workers and technicians; (4) supervisors, technicians, and skilled blue-collar workers; (5) less-skilled blue-collar, sales, and service workers; and (6) farmers and farm laborers. In addition to those who are gainfully employed, four other groups are represented: the unemployed, the retired, those keeping house, and those not in the labor force.

The Department of Labor has developed an elaborate occupational code that divides types of work into various categories: managers, profes-sional and technical, administrative support and sales, skilled blue-collar, less-skilled blue-collar, service, and farmers/laborers. These major occupational categories seem self-evident but are less so when looked at more closely. For example, consider the following list of occupations: accountants, musicians, airplane pilots, and stockbrokers. Many people would probably consider all of these professional jobs because of their pay and educational requirements. However, of these, only musicians are officially categorized as professionals, while all of the others are put in different categories: accountants are placed with managers, airplane pilots with technicians, and stockbrokers with other sales workers.

So, while the official categories appear to represent a hierarchical listing of "good" and "bad" jobs, occupations with high and low skills and high and low pay have been lumped together. Thus, for our purposes, we have come up with simpler and more similar commonsense categorizations. In particular, we have tried to remedy four major incongruities in the official code where occupations with very different pay and educational requirements are combined together. In the official code:

1. Managers at fast-food restaurants and retail establishments are not distinguished from corporate vice presidents; here, they are listed with nonprofessional supervisors.

2. Stock and real estate brokers are combined with sales clerks even though brokers must have college degrees, earn many times

more, and work far longer hours than sales clerks. To correct this we include sales reps and brokers with other business professionals.

3. Police and firefighters—municipal employees who fit more in the craft model of organization and skill—are alongside janitors, fast-food workers, and health aides. We have assigned them to the group that includes skilled blue-collar craft, machine, and repair workers.

4. Medical and science laboratory workers, operators of numerical control equipment, and paralegals are often grouped with managers and professionals. These workers are highly skilled but not as much as other professionals; nor do they have the same autonomy, pay, or education. As they more closely resemble other moderately paid workers such as supervisors, craft and repair workers, police, and firefighters, we combine these occupations into the same group.

Figure 14 presents the income profiles of the first five occupation groups (the farming occupations are excluded because they are such a small group). In order to accommodate the very high incomes at the top of the manager-doctor-lawyer occupation group, the incomes at the lower percentiles look closer than they really are. For example, the median income of the top occupation group is $128,000 versus $108,000 for other professionals, about $78,000 for the medium-skilled occupations, and $52,000 for the lowest-skilled occupations. The gap is largest at the 10th percentile, where the top occupations have an income of $54,000 (actually higher than the median of the bottom group) versus just $11,000 for the bottom occupation group.

These income figures show that the higher earnings of the different occupations translate into more marriages and more partners with high earnings.

The two middle-skill occupations have a very similar income profile even though the supervisors and skilled blue-collar workers have much higher earnings than the clerical and technician group. The first group tends to be mainly men while the second group tends to be mainly women. But the earnings gaps between these two groups don't translate into income differences because the women are married to moderate-earning males, while the men are married to lower-earning females.

Figure 15 shows the income distributions of adults who are currently not working. Of this group, nonworking wives of unretired husbands have the highest incomes with a median value of $52,223. While this is a reasonable amount of size-adjusted income, it contrasts with an overall median of $66,260 and a whopping median of $77,850 for husband-wife couples. Of nonretired couples, 5 percent have no earners, 35 percent have one earner, and the majority (60 percent) has both husband and wife with a job. Not surprisingly, the median incomes of these groups vary tremendously: $28,000 for zero earners (they could have been working at some point in the previous year), $63,000 for one earner, and $100,000 for two earners.

Two-earner couples are obviously the most successful household type, and they differ from the rest

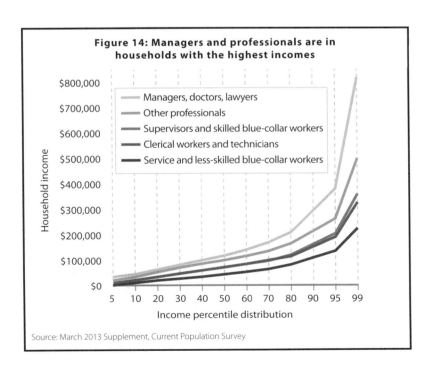

Figure 14: Managers and professionals are in households with the highest incomes

Household income (y-axis): $0 to $800,000

Legend:
Managers, doctors, lawyers
Other professionals
Supervisors and skilled blue-collar workers
Clerical workers and technicians
Service and less-skilled blue-collar workers

Income percentile distribution (x-axis): 5, 10, 20, 30, 40, 50, 60, 70, 80, 90, 95, 99

Source: March 2013 Supplement, Current Population Survey

of the population in terms of education. Of these couples, only 18 percent have neither husband nor wife with at least some college attendance. In terms of highest education in the household, the majority has at least one member with a BA (30 percent with a BA and 24 percent with a graduate degree). And once again, education matters: for couples and partners whose highest attainment is a high school diploma, their median income is $50,000; with some college but no four-year degree, a median of $73,000; with a BA as highest attainment, $102,000; and with a graduate degree, $135,000.

Of the other groups that are not employed, the ones with the lowest incomes (median income of just over $22,000) are those "not in the labor force" but not retired or unemployed. Many of these people are disabled, on welfare, or living as a roommate while not even looking for work.

Finally, retired people and the unemployed have very similar income profiles, although they have different ways of reaching this income. More than half of unemployed people live with people who are working, and often their spell of unemployment is not that long. The tragedy of long-term unemployment (over six months) has reached very high levels during the Great Recession and the subsequent slow recovery. For most unemployed people, however, unemployment typically lasts two to four months, and often their new jobs pay less than their former jobs. Those who don't get a job during the first six months are stigmatized, in that employers see this long period of unemployment and assume there is a reason that has to do with the person and not the economy. In a world where hiring is an imperfect art, any condition out of the ordinary can be given great weight.

Retired people, on the other hand, get their cash incomes from Social Security, pensions, payments or annuities from retirement savings accounts, and returns on past savings (often in the form of stocks and bonds). They also receive a very valuable asset in the form of cheap or free Medicare. Furthermore, they have fewer expenses because they often have paid off their mortgages, have a full complement of home furnishings and appliances, don't have expenses associated with commuting to work, and often can downsize their expectations. Consequently, in surveys by the Employment Benefits and Retirement Institute, a large majority of retired people report that they are living as well as they did in their early fifties (a time when they had considerably more money coming in).

Like many things in our economy, the living conditions of the elderly are very unequal, with a sizable proportion receiving low Social Security payments and barely eking by. Sometimes they are able to get help from their adult children, but this puts pressure on people who don't have abundant resources. This has led to a new term, the "sandwich generation," to describe adults who have to simultaneously support their children and their parents.

Nonetheless, when looked at historically, the current condition of the elderly is quite good. In 1960, 35 percent of seniors lived in poverty, even though roughly half of the men were still in the labor force. Today, the poverty rate among the elderly has declined to 10 percent, and fewer than 30 percent of elderly men remain in the labor force. These improved conditions are largely due to the expansion and increased generosity of Social

Figure 15: Of those now working, wives have highest incomes

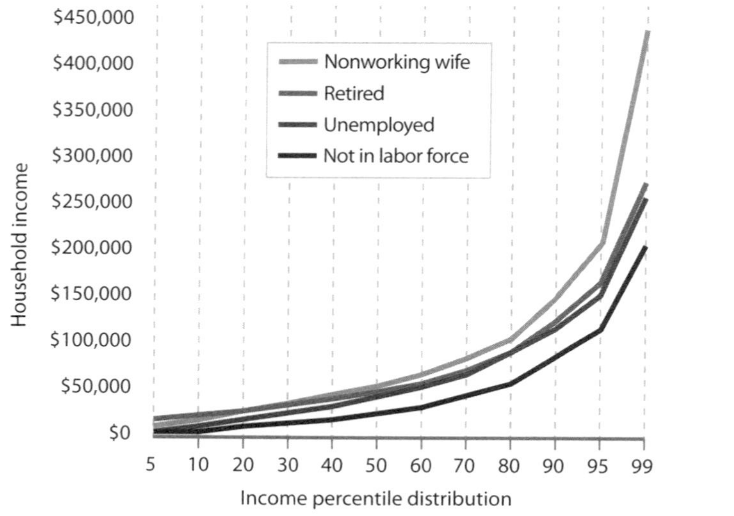

Legend:
- Nonworking wife
- Retired
- Unemployed
- Not in labor force

Y-axis: Household income ($0 to $450,000)
X-axis: Income percentile distribution (5, 10, 20, 30, 40, 50, 60, 70, 80, 90, 95, 99)

Source: March 2013 Supplement, Current Population Survey

TABLE 13:
DISTRIBUTION OF EDUCATION WITHIN OCCUPATIONS AND LABOR FORCE STATUS IF NOT WORKING

	Less than High school	High School	Some college or AA degree	BA degree	Graduate degree	All
Managers, doctors, lawyers (%)	2	14	21	30	33	100
Other professionals (%)	1	7	19	43	30	100
Supervisors and skilled blue-collar workers (%)	10	36	33	17	4	100
Clerical workers and technicians (%)	3	28	43	21	5	100
Service and less-skilled blue-collar workers (%)	18	41	30	9	2	100
Farmers and farm laborers (%)	20	37	24	14	5	100
Unemployed (%)	16	34	30	14	6	100
Retired (%)	17	36	24	14	10	100
Not in labor force (%)	19	33	32	12	5	100
Nonworking wife of nonretired husband (%)	16	31	26	19	7	100

Security and private pension plans—nearly half of Social Security recipients would be classified as poor without their monthly retirement checks.

There is some concern that future retirees won't live as well as current retirees. Business retirement policies have changed considerably over the past twenty years as defined contribution plans (401(k) and similar individual retirement accounts) have replaced company pensions (called defined benefit plans). Pensions work very well for workers who stay with the same company for over twenty years because of the vesting requirements and the formulas that reward longevity and high pay at the end of one's career.

Therefore, anyone who moves from company to company will likely do better under a 401(k) plan than a company pension. Companies prefer the defined contribution approach because they aren't subject to investment risk (returns on the portfolio turn out to be lower than expected) and longevity risk (people collect benefits longer than expected). While many individuals will theoretically do better under a defined contribution plan, there are three problems that make this less likely: they don't contribute as much as they should and often pass up some of the employer match; they borrow from their plans and hence can lose some of the principal and return; and they aren't good investors, often choosing low-return strategies and moving from plan to plan.

Occupations, Labor Force Status, and Education

As Table 13 shows, the education distribution of the various occupations and labor force statuses reflect the different income levels. The two top occupations have a much higher share of people with a BA or greater. The top category has many

TABLE 14:
MORE EDUCATION LEADS TO BETTER JOBS

	Less than High school	HS diploma or GED	Some college or AA degree	BA degree	Graduate degree
Managers, Doctors, Lawyers	1%	4%	6%	12%	23%
Other Professionals	1%	4%	11%	33%	41%
Supervisors and Skilled Blue-Collar Workers	11%	15%	15%	10%	4%
Clerical Workers and Technicians	3%	9%	15%	10%	4%
Service and Less Skilled Blue-Collar Workers	25%	22%	17%	7%	2%
Farmers and Farm Laborers	1%	1%	1%	0%	0%
Unemployed	6%	5%	4%	3%	2%
Retired	30%	25%	17%	13%	16%
Not in Labor Force	12%	8%	8%	4%	3%
Nonworking wife of nonretired husband	11%	8%	7%	7%	5%
	100%	100%	100%	100%	100%

more managers (an occupation that doesn't require a graduate or even a BA degree) than doctors and lawyers (occupations that do require a graduate degree). Consequently, the teachers, accountants, social workers, and writers who are part of the other professional category actually have a greater proportion with a BA (73 percent) than managers, doctors, and lawyers have (63 percent).

Among middle-skill jobs, the ones that are held predominantly by women (clerical workers and technicians) have many fewer people with at most a high school diploma (31 percent) than the skilled blue-collar and supervisor jobs that are held predominantly by men (46 percent). By contrast, retail, services, and less-skilled blue-collar jobs have the lowest concentration of workers with at least a BA (11 percent) and 59 percent with high school diploma or less. The farming occupation and the four categories of nonworkers have more or less similar education profiles—about 50 percent with at most

high school, 20 percent with a BA or graduate degree, and 30 percent with some college, a certificate, or two-year degree.

Another way to look at these data is to have the columns instead of the rows add to 100 percent (Table 14). This shows where workers with different levels of education are employed. For example, 64 percent of graduate-degree holders are in the top two groups of managers and professionals, another 16 percent are retired, and 5 percent are nonworking wives, leaving just 15 percent for the other occupations and out-of-the-labor-force categories. Those with a bachelor's degree have very good profiles as well: 45 percent are managers and professionals, 13 percent are retired, and 7 percent are nonworking wives. This leaves over a third in other jobs (mainly middle-skill jobs) or out of the labor force.

Switching to the other end of the educational ladder, very few are in managerial and professional jobs (just 2 percent), while another 14 percent are in middle-skill jobs. Fully 30 percent are retired, reflecting the fact that the older cohorts were educated when fewer people went to college. Another 30 percent were not working, and 25 percent were in retail, service, and less-skilled manual jobs.

In today's world, it is rare for those with just a high school diploma to make it into the top rungs of managerial and professional jobs (8 percent). The remainder of high-school-only people are retired (25 percent), in middle-skill jobs (24 percent), in less-skilled jobs (23 percent), or other categories of not working (21 percent).

Finally, there is a step up—and more variety in status—for the group that has some college or a two-year associates of arts degree: 17 percent in managerial and professional jobs, 30 percent in middle-skill jobs, 23 percent in low-skilled jobs, 24 percent being retired or nonworking wives, and 13 percent being unemployed or not in the labor force at all.

The Status of Women

LOOKING MORE CLOSELY AT THE DETAILED occupations within the six occupation categories used on the poster, there are many jobs that tend to be dominated either by male or female workers. First, among employed nondependent adults, 15 percent of men and 11 percent of women are senior business managers, doctors, or lawyers. Among our category of other professionals, women tend to be employed as teachers, social workers, and registered nurses, with men as engineers, sales representatives, and other senior business professionals. Next, among middle-skill jobs, women work in offices and as health care technicians and aides (the third occupation category), while men are concentrated as supervisors, skilled blue-collar workers, police, and firefighters (our fourth category). Finally, there is another gender split among the fifth and sixth occupation groups: while women work as sales clerks and low-skill service workers, men are much more prevalent as factory operatives and laborers.

This is not a neutral division of labor because the pay scales for workers with similar education are vastly different. In the 1970s and 1980s, female activists publicized the earnings "gender gap" and demanded "equal pay for equal work." Since men and women were mostly in different jobs, it was not clear what "equal work" meant, so the follow-up demand was for "comparable worth" pay scales in different occupations.

Court victories and increasing women's labor force attachment increased women's earnings considerably. Yet, the most commonly cited gender gap figure today is 23 percent (women earn 77 percent of what men do). This ratio is based on comparing the median earnings of male and female workers who worked full-time for a single year. The work experiences of many low-paid women are excluded because they do not meet the full-time, full-year standard. This is justified by arguing that only workers with strong labor force participation should be used for this comparison. Further, hourly pay rather than annual earnings is used to make the pay-for-work unit as homogeneous as possible.

Rose and Hartmann (2004), however, show that the earnings gender gap is much greater when a long-term perspective is taken. Table 14 shows that prime-age women are much less likely to be active labor market participants for fifteen out of fifteen years in their prime working years: 84 percent of men and 48 percent of women met this standard in the period from 1983 through 1998. Reflecting women's increased labor force attachment, the comparable figures for the 1968–1982 period were 87 percent of men and just 28 percent of women.[14]

It should be noted that for both men and women the costs of being out of the labor force even temporarily are very high. Even if only one year is missed out of fifteen, the yearly earnings of those with this break are over 30 percent lower than for

14. The Panel Study on Income Dynamics, the data source used for this analysis, can't be updated because it switched to collecting data every other year. Nonetheless, these results are probably reasonably accurate, in terms of percentage ratios, to what exists today.

TABLE 15:
THE LONG-TERM LABOR MARKET EXPERIENCE OF WOMEN AND MEN: EARNINGS, WORK HOURS, AND YEARS OUT OF THE LABOR FORCE, 1983–1998
[15-year averages*]

Number of years out of labor force	Share (%)	Annual earnings	Annual hours	Hourly wage	Hourly wage ratio
FEMALES (WEIGHTED POPULATION = 33.9 MILLION)					
All (aged 26–59)	100.0	$21,363	1,498	$12.82	60.0
None	48.4	$29,507	1,766	$15.72	69.6
1	10.2	$19,341	1,513	$12.25	72.3
2 or 3	11.8	$14,868	1,376	$10.56	75.6
4 or more	29.5	$11,280	1,100	$9.25	63.8
MALES (WEIGHTED POPULATION = 32.7 MILLION)					
All (aged 26–59)	100.0	$49,068	2,219	$21.38	
None	84.0	$52,510	2,260	$22.60	
1	7.5	$36,867	2,210	$16.94	
2 or 3	4.8	$28,777	2,062	$13.97	
4 or more	3.7	$21,896	1,524	$14.50	

* Zero-earnings years are not included; i.e., averages for earnings and hours are calculated only for years when work is reported. Weighted data are used to calculate all figures.

SOURCE: PANEL STUDY OF INCOME DYNAMICS

those without an interruption. Apparently, this single-year break has large consequences for one's career progression. Under all circumstances, women work many fewer hours per year when working than do comparable men.

But even among workers who worked fifteen out of fifteen years, there are considerably more men (Table 15). Of this group, 11 percent of men but 45 percent of women averaged less than $25,000 per year. Among the lowest earnings group (less than $15,000 per year), 90 percent were female workers.

Using a long-term perspective, the gender gap can be computed in different ways (Table 16). If all workers are included, women's total earnings

over fifteen years were 62 percent lower than those of comparable men with 40 percent of the difference being due to hours worked. This total earnings approach is important because it is the basis for earning Social Security benefits on the basis of one's own labor market experience.

The gender gap could also be computed as:

- 57 percent on the basis of comparing earnings only for years in which a worker had positive earnings;
- 44 percent on the basis of comparing workers with earnings in fifteen out of fifteen years; and
- 36 percent on the basis of comparing

workers with the strongest connection to the labor market (working fifteen out of fifteen years and working at least 1,750 hours in at least twelve years).

Even though the earnings gap is large, the family income gap is much smaller: over fifteen years, men's average family income was $67,000 versus women's average of $61,000. However, among adults who were rarely married (at most two out of fifteen years), men's average family income was $57,000 while women's average was $41,000. These numbers indicate that women's decisions are conditioned by their need to have time available for family responsibilities.

The system is self-reinforcing. First, since women make less than men, it makes more sense for women to forgo working than their husbands or male partners. Second, since companies expect women to periodically need to leave work, wom-

TABLE 16:
THE DISTRIBUTION OF AVERAGE ANNUAL EARNINGS AMONG WOMEN AND MEN WITH STRONG LABOR FORCE ATTACHMENT, 1983–1998

| Average annual earnings | PERCENT DISTRIBUTION | | | Women as a percent of total |
	Women	Men	Total	
All (aged 26–59)	100.0	100.0	100.0	36.7
Less than $15,000	17.4	1.3	8.3	90.1
$15,000–$25,000	27.2	9.5	17.2	68.7
$25,000–$50,000	45.9	45.1	45.4	43.9
$50,000–$75,000	8.3	29.7	20.4	17.7
More than $75,000	1.3	14.4	8.7	6.5

TABLE 17:
MEASURES AND SOURCES OF THE LONG-TERM GENDER GAP, 1983–1998

| Population in comparison | AVERAGE ANNUAL EARNINGS | | Earnings ratio | Earnings gap | Gap adjusted for hours worked |
	Women	Men			
All workers with at least one year with earnings, counting zero-earnings years	$18,239	$48,178	37.9	62.1	36
All workers with at least one year with earnings, excluding zero-earnings years	$21,363	$49,068	43.5	56.5	35
All workers with earnings in every year	$29,507	$52,510	56.2	43.8	28
All workers with earnings every year and full-time work (1,750 hours or more) in 12 of 15 years	$34,915	$54,188	64.4	35.6	28

en's jobs are created that are structured to have workers come and go more often. Third, these jobs will tend to pay less even for workers who don't take periodic leaves because the companies don't know which women will leave because of family responsibilities and which women won't. Fourth, companies will be less likely to spend money to train female workers or to put them on fast-moving career tracks. Fifth, young women will set their aspirations often in response to the role models that they see.

This system is predicated on women being married to a male breadwinner. Whenever women don't have a male earner present, their limited earnings will have severe consequences on their family income.

Conclusion: Challenges of the New Economy

MANY AMERICANS ARE WORRIED. THEY SEE an economy out of balance, with low-skill, low-pay, dead-end service jobs replacing the good, high-paying manufacturing jobs of the past. They wonder where the middle-class jobs of the future will come from.

At the same time that the share of service employment has grown, there has been a remarkable upgrading in the skills of the workforce as more people have gotten a college education. Further, as was shown above, the college wage premium in the United States (the difference between average college and high-school wages) grew as well: the earnings premium for workers with a bachelor's degree over workers with just a high-school diploma jumped from 40 percent in 1980 to about 80 percent today.

How can we square the success of college-educated workers with the popular portrait of a service economy replete with low-skill, dead-end "McJobs"? The answer is that the conventional wisdom doesn't provide an answer.

Let's start with a simple exercise. Look around any central city today and you will see one large office building after another. Go to the inner suburbs and you will see even more office buildings. At the airports of many cities (which can be twenty to forty minutes out of town), there are yet more such buildings. But when pundits and politicians talk about jobs and employment, they talk about "manufacturing" and "services," only rarely mentioning offices, despite their obvious and huge role in our economy.

To clarify this debate, I developed an alternative framework that reworked the traditional occupational and industrial categories into "functional groups" (Rose 2010). The five functions are: extractive production (agriculture, fishing, mining, etc.), industrial production (manufacturing, transportation, and construction), low-skilled services (retail and food and personal services), high-skilled services (employment in education, health care, and communications), and administration and coordination (including all front-office activities, finance and related industries, business and professional services, and public administration).

While the office economy has been around for a while, few researchers have estimated the size of this sector because it is spread out among many different industries. In the traditional approach, the front offices of factories, mines, hospitals, and the like are included with the primary industrial content of the activity. In the functional approach, each occupation within each industry is allocated to one of the five functions. For example, in manufacturing, the direct production workers are put in industrial production, while the managers and clerical workers are classified as office workers.

The five functions can be grouped into three grand categories: the first two represent manual labor on farms, in factories, at construction sites, and in other similar types of activities. The third function is low-skilled services and is what people think of when they talk about dead-end jobs.

The final two are what I call the "high-end post-industrial service economy" and are rarely talked about because somehow they are considered too small to make a difference.

As Figure 16 shows, there has been a large decline in manufacturing and related blue-collar tasks, a rise in high-end services, and no change in low-skill services. Office and related work went from 34 percent of employment in 1960 to 43 percent in 2013, while employment in health care, education, and communications went from 10 to 21 percent over the same period. This combined increase of 18 percentage points was offset by declines in the share of manufacturing and related activities (31 to 15 percent) and of agriculture and related work (6 to 2 percent). Another surprise is the narrow range of the share of employment in low-skill services from a low of 18.9 to a high of 20.3 percent.

To emphasize the point, *the high-end service sector is the main driver of our economy today*. It is responsible for 64 percent of employment, 74 percent of earnings (workers in this category make 46 percent more than workers in the other three functional areas—$51,800 versus $35,400), employ 81 percent of all those with a bachelor's degree and 91 percent of those with graduate degrees.

These figures should not be surprising for anyone who has a realistic view of what makes the economy go around. In a 2014, I used input-output analysis to show how everything was produced in terms of industries, occupations, earnings, and education of the workforce. What most people don't realize is that basically half of the final price of goods and services bought by consumers comes from intermediate producers far removed from producing and selling the product.

For example, consider the $1.3 trillion we spend each year on food and drink. In today's economy, just 16 percent of the final price of all food purchases goes to produce this output: farmers (5 percent), food manufacturers like Dole, Del Monte, and General Foods (7 percent), and imported agricultural products (4 percent). A slightly bigger proportion (19 percent) goes for advertising, banking and legal services, insurance, real estate, and other business services. Then of course there are restaurants (18 percent), grocery stores (9 percent), transportation and wholesaling (9 percent), and a variety of other sources including other manufacturers (e.g., those producing the refrigerators and other fixtures in stores and restaurants), utility costs for the public spaces and the transportation, and smaller contributions from other sources.

One hundred years ago, the lion's share of food production would have gone to farmers, with food manufacturers, trade, and transportation splitting the rest. As recently as 1967, 30 percent of food output was connected to producing the food: farmers (14 percent), food manufacturers (12 percent), and just 8 percent for finance, advertising, real estate, and other business services. This shift to a smaller role for the direct producers (manufacturers and farmers) and an increased role of business services conducted in offices occurred throughout the economy as productivity increased output while reducing the share of the workforce involved in producing things.

In terms of occupations, I've developed a simple three-tier categorization:

Elite jobs: all managers and professionals;

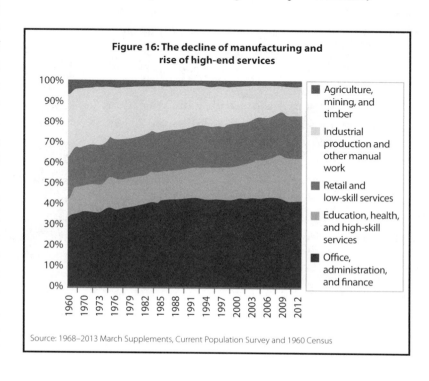

Figure 16: The decline of manufacturing and rise of high-end services

- Agriculture, mining, and timber
- Industrial production and other manual work
- Retail and low-skill services
- Education, health, and high-skill services
- Office, administration, and finance

Source: 1968–2013 March Supplements, Current Population Survey and 1960 Census

Good jobs: supervisors, skilled blue-collar and craft workers, technicians, police, firefighters, and clerical workers; and

Less-skilled jobs: blue-collar machine operators and laborers, sales clerks, and a variety of "service" workers such as guards, restaurant and fast food workers, janitors, shoe repairers, and bus and truck drivers.

Contrary to many claims about the growth in low-skilled services, the quality of employment in America has been shifting upward during the past forty years. In 1960, almost one-half of the workforce (44 percent) was in less-skilled positions and only 18 percent held elite jobs. By 2013, the less-skilled share had declined by 16 percentage points to 28 percent. While the share of middle-skill good jobs declined mildly (from 39 to 35 percent), the big gainer was the more than doubling of the top tier from 17 to 37 percent.

As documented above, university attendance grew by leaps and bounds over these years. In the 1960s, college degrees were mainly for the clergy, teachers, and some professionals. As the number of university graduates has grown, these degrees became a prerequisite for those who went into business as managers or professionals (e.g., accountants, insurance agents, stock and real estate brokers, and sales representatives). While some think that this is just credential inflation, those with BA degrees in these jobs earn over 50 percent more in the same occupations. This premium demonstrates that those with more education are able to translate the higher skills into higher earnings.

The simultaneous rise in the share of the workforce that is college educated and of the earnings premiums that the most educated have over those with just a high school diploma shows how much our high-end service economy has changed. Using a supply-and-demand framework, Goldin and Katz (2008) demonstrate that these facts are only consistent with a large rise in the demand for college-level skills. And there is every reason to believe that these forces are going to continue in the future. Going forward, it will be hard to earn middle-class wages without some form of post-secondary education or training. For many, this will be a two-year, four-year, or graduate degree. Others will get a vocational or technical certificate from a public community college or from a private business, technical, or vocational school.

The path one takes is affected greatly by how well one did as a student in high school. Those who get low Bs and Cs will have difficulty getting any sort of college degree. If more students are going to earn a college degree, the quality of graduating high school seniors will have to increase.

As America continues to drag itself painfully out of recession, doubts have emerged about our economic future. The world is constantly changing and is more globally integrated than ever. Fears are rampant that our economic structure, with our huge service sector and our relatively low levels of employment in manufacturing, is fundamentally out of balance and cannot produce the kinds of jobs Americans need.

This pessimistic view lacks historical perspective. In 1958, John Kenneth Galbraith saw an economy that was producing more goods and services than ever before and celebrated this triumph over want and deprivation in his book *The Affluent Society*.[15] By comparison with recent times, that standard of living was pretty paltry: In 1957, GDP per person was $15,187 in 2005 dollars versus $42,926 in 2007. Despite our affluence, we may not feel like we are living with much more because our expectations are so high (86 percent of Americans have cell phones) and our standards have changed over time. When the suburban development of Levittown—considered a model for subsequent suburban development—opened in the early 1950s, the average home size was less than 1,000 square feet; today, newly constructed homes are more than double this size, with air-conditioning and many other standard features that were once considered luxuries. At the same time, of course, the increasingly unequal distribution of economic gains since roughly 1979 has slowed the growth of living standards for many Americans outside the famous 1 percent.

15. Paperback version reprinted in 1998 by Mariner Books (a division of Houghton Mifflin Harcourt).

For all that, people seem to be aware of long-term economic gains: the biannual General Social Survey always asks the following question: "Compared with your parents at the same age, is your standard of living better, the same, or worse?" Consistently, about 65 percent say better, 20 percent say the same, and 15 percent say worse. During the past two surveys, the Great Recession showed its effect in responses to this question, but it was relatively modest, with the share saying "better" dropping into the low 60s.

No single conclusion can be drawn from this presentation of social and education stratification in America. Most people tend to associate with others like themselves, assuming that incomes throughout the country are concentrated in a bulky middle, with themselves somewhere near the center. Go to an exclusive suburban high school and ask students what percentile a family making $150,000 a year falls into, and you will probably be told something between the 60th and 80th percentiles—considerably below the 90th percentile, which is the case. Conversely, many residents of inner cities are likely to think that the median family income lies somewhere between $35,000 and $50,000. In other words, what you take from this picture of the United States may depend on your preconceptions.

The long ribbons of color and variety of household composition on the poster reflect the diversity within the United States today. Rather than a homogeneous middle class, which would take the shape of a closely bunched bell curve, the income profile is more columnlike, with a long, narrowing band extending upward.

These material differences tell only part of the story, though. Workers in top white-collar jobs have much greater autonomy than blue-collar workers; for the former, supervision is indirect, but for the latter it is very direct. Not only do job satisfaction and sense of self-worth vary, but studies also show that blue-collar workers face many more workplace hazards, experience more on-the-job stress, and are much more prone to all sorts of diseases. Most service workers and low-level clerical and sales workers also face close supervision, job insecurity, and limited possibilities for promotion.

These distinctions (and there are others) make it clear that the widespread use of the term "middle class" is probably inappropriate. Because it includes practically all Americans, it has lost its descriptive value; indeed, it obscures vast differences in lifestyles, community, working conditions, and political outlook. It is important to develop categories that can more accurately and meaningfully describe the features that distinguish groups from one another. This becomes particularly important in the face of the uneven economic record of the past fifteen years: college-educated professionals and managers have moved ahead while others have stagnated or even lost ground.

To develop such categories requires detailed analyses. All too frequently, this work has been left to experts, because they are the only ones equipped to understand the data. We hope this poster and book will change this by making information more accessible. But this work presents only a limited picture of contemporary society, one that focuses mainly on income and occupation. The issues surrounding expectations, quality of life, and political involvement (to mention just a few) are lacking.

Describing social conditions is very complex; the poster and accompanying text are meant to be introductions to this topic. As stated earlier, the purpose of this work is not to provide "answers" but stimulate thought and more questions.

Appendix I

Combining Income, Educational Level, and Family Status to Create the Figures on the Poster

THE AMERICAN SOCIAL STRUCTURE IS VERY complex with a variety of common and rare household types—1,000 icons can never fully represent 200 million people. The poster is created by computing a series of distributions:

- the shares of independent adults in types of households;

- the distribution of four race/ethnicity categories that are then each divided into the five household types;

- the distribution of households by income across the distribution from zero to one million dollars; and

- the distribution of educational attainment connected to four race/ethnicity catego-

ries, two genders, six household types, and eight levels of household income.

After all these distributions are computed, specific icons are created showing gender, household status, income, education, and race/ethnicity. Since the world does not fall neatly into 200,000 person chunks, there are many possibilities that have only a small percentage of a full icon. All of these "partial icons" have to be defined to satisfy in a way that satisfies the overall distributions. There is no one solution to solving this problem, even though the overall distributions are always correct.

The following ten tables give the exact definition of each icon as it appears on the poster. The first five are the different types of households by race, education, and income, while the last five tables matches the education of husbands and wives by income level.

INCOMES OF HUSBANDS BY EDUCATIONAL LEVEL (BY ICONS ON THE POSTER)

	INCOME IN THOUSANDS OF DOLLARS								
	$0–20	$20–40	$40–60	$60–80	$80–100	$100–125	$125–150	$►150	Total
All races	22	52	53	51	42	40	25	55	340
Non-Hispanic whites	3	6	1	2	1	1	1	0	15
Less than high school	4	14	16	12	11	6	3	5	71
High school	2	8	10	11	10	10	4	8	63
Some college	2	4	5	7	7	9	7	16	57
BA degree	1	1	4	4	3	4	4	15	36
Graduate degree	12	33	36	36	32	30	19	44	242
Total									
Non-Hispanic African Americans									
Less than high school	1	1	1						3
High school	1	3	1	3		1	1		10
Some college	1	1	2	1	1	1	1		8
BA degree			1		1	1		1	4
Graduate degree					1			1	2
Total	3	5	5	4	3	3	2	2	27
Hispanics									
Less than high school	3	6	4	2	1				16
High school	2	3	3	3	1	1	1		14
Some college	1	1	2	2	1	1	1	1	10
BA degree		1		1	1	1		1	5
Graduate degree						1		1	2
Total	6	11	9	8	4	4	2	3	47
Asian and other races									
Less than high school		1	1						2
High school	1		1	1	1	1			5
Some college		1		1	1	1		1	5
BA degree			1	1	1		1	2	6
Graduate degree		1				1	1	3	6
Total	1	3	3	3	3	3	2	6	24

INCOMES OF SINGLE MEN BY EDUCATIONAL LEVEL
(BY ICONS ON THE POSTER)

INCOME IN THOUSANDS OF DOLLARS

	$0–20	$20–40	$40–60	$60–80	$80–100	$100–125	$125–150	$▸150	Total
All races	37	31	19	10	4	3	2	3	109
Non-Hispanic whites									
Less than high school	4	1	0	0	0	0	0	0	5
High school	7	6	4	2	1	0	0	1	21
Some college	7	7	4	3	0	1	0	0	22
BA degree	3	5	5	2	0	1	1	1	18
Graduate degree	1	2	1	1	1	0	1	1	8
Total	22	21	14	8	2	2	2	3	74
Non-Hispanic African Americans									
Less than high school	2								2
High school	2	2	1						5
Some college	2	1	1						4
BA degree		1			1				2
Graduate degree				1					1
Total	6	4	2	1	1	0	0	0	14
Hispanics									
Less than high school	3	2							5
High school	2	2							4
Some college	1	1	1						3
BA degree					1				1
Graduate degree									0
Total	6	5	1	0	1	0	0	0	13
Asian and other races									
Less than high school			1						1
High school	1								1
Some college	1	1							2
BA degree	1			1					2
Graduate degree			1			1			2
Total	3	1	2	1	0	1	0	0	8

Appendix Table 3:
INCOMES OF SINGLE WOMEN BY EDUCATIONAL LEVEL
(BY ICONS ON THE POSTER)

INCOME IN THOUSANDS OF DOLLARS

	$0–20	$20–40	$40–60	$60–80	$80–100	$100–125	$125–150	$▸150	Total
All races	50	32	16	8	4	2	1	1	114
Non-Hispanic whites									
Less than high school	6	2	0	0	0	0	0	0	8
High school	12	8	1	1	0	1	0	0	23
Some college	10	6	5	2	1	0	0	1	25
BA degree	4	6	3	3	1	0	0	0	17
Graduate degree	1	2	2	1	1	1	1	0	9
Total	33	24	11	7	3	2	1	1	82
Non-Hispanic African Americans									
Less than high school	2	1							3
High school	3	1	1						5
Some college	2	2	1						5
BA degree	1				1				2
Graduate degree	1			1					2
Total	9	4	2	1	1	0	0	0	17
Hispanics									
Less than high school	2								2
High school	1	1							2
Some college	1	1							2
BA degree		1	1						2
Graduate degree			1						1
Total	4	3	2	0	0	0	0	0	9
Asian and other races									
Less than high school	1								1
High school	1								1
Some college	1	1							2
BA degree	1		1						2
Graduate degree									0
Total	4	1	1	0	0	0	0	0	6

INCOMES OF MALE-HEADED HOUSEHOLDS BY EDUCATIONAL LEVEL (BY ICONS ON THE POSTER)

INCOME IN THOUSANDS OF DOLLARS

	$0–20	$20–40	$40–60	$60–80	$80–100	$100–125	$125–150	$▸150	Total
All races	4	7	5	3	2	2	1	2	26
Non-Hispanic whites									
Less than high school	O	O	1	O	O	O	O	O	1
High school	O	2	1	1	O	1	O	O	5
Some college	1	1	O	2	O	O	1	O	5
BA degree	1	1	O	O	O	O	O	O	2
Graduate degree	O	O	O	O	O	O	O	1	1
Total	2	4	2	3	O	1	1	1	14
Non-Hispanic African Americans									
Less than high school		1							1
High school	1								1
Some college			1						1
BA degree						1			1
Graduate degree									O
Total	1	1	1	O	O	1	O	O	4
Hispanics									
Less than high school	1						1		2
High school			1		1				2
Some college		1							1
BA degree									O
Graduate degree									O
Total	1	1	1	O	1	O	O	1	5
Asian and other races									
Less than high school		1							1
High school			1						1
Some college									O
BA degree					1				1
Graduate degree	O								O
Total	O	1	1	O	1	O	O	O	3

INCOMES OF FEMALE-HEADED HOUSEHOLDS BY EDUCATIONAL LEVEL (BY ICONS ON THE POSTER)

INCOME IN THOUSANDS OF DOLLARS

	$0–20	$20–40	$40–60	$60–80	$80–100	$100–125	$125–150	$►150	Total
All races	22	20	12	7	4	2	2	2	71
Non-Hispanic whites									
Less than high school	1	1	1	1	0	0	0	0	4
High school	3	3	2	1	1	0	0	0	10
Some college	4	3	1	2	1	0	1	0	12
BA degree	1	1	2	0	1	1	0	0	6
Graduate degree	0	1	1	0	0	0	0	0	2
Total	9	9	7	4	3	1	1	0	34
Non-Hispanic African Americans									
Less than high school	2					1			3
High school	3	2	1						6
Some college	2	3	2						7
BA degree		1						1	2
Graduate degree				1					1
Total	7	6	3	1	0	1	0	1	19
Hispanics									
Less than high school	3	1							4
High school	1	2	1						4
Some college	1	1	1		1				4
BA degree				1					1
Graduate degree								1	1
Total	5	4	2	1	1	0	0	1	14
Asian and other races									
Less than high school	1			1					2
High school		1							1
Some college							1		1
BA degree									0
Graduate degree									0
Total	1	1	0	1	0	0	1	0	4

APPENDIX TABLE 6:
INCOMES OF MARRIED COUPLES, HUSBAND HAS LESS THAN HIGH SCHOOL DIPLOMA (BY ICONS ON THE POSTER)

	INCOME IN THOUSANDS OF DOLLARS								
	$0–20	$20–40	$40–60	$60–80	$80–100	$100–125	$125–150	$▸150	Total
Less than high school	4	7	4	2	1	0	0	0	18
High school	2	5	2	0	1	0	1	0	11
Some college	1	2	1	1	0	1	0	0	6
BA degree	0	0	0	1	0	0	0	0	1
Graduate degree	0	0	0	0	0	0	0	0	0
Total	7	14	7	4	2	1	1	0	36

APPENDIX TABLE 7:
INCOMES OF MARRIED COUPLES, HUSBAND HAS HIGH SCHOOL DIPLOMA (BY ICONS ON THE POSTER)

	INCOME IN THOUSANDS OF DOLLARS								
	$0–20	$20–40	$40–60	$60–80	$80–100	$100–125	$125–150	$▸150	Total
Less than high school	1	3	2	2	1	0	0	0	9
High school	5	11	11	11	5	4	2	2	51
Some college	1	5	6	5	4	2	2	1	26
BA degree	1	1	2	0	2	2	1	1	10
Graduate degree	0	0	0	1	1	1	0	1	4
Total	8	20	21	19	13	9	5	5	100

APPENDIX TABLE 8:
INCOMES OF MARRIED COUPLES, HUSBAND HAS SOME COLLEGE OR TWO-YEAR DEGREE (BY ICONS ON THE POSTER)

	INCOME IN THOUSANDS OF DOLLARS								
	$0–20	$20–40	$40–60	$60–80	$80–100	$100–125	$125–150	$▸150	Total
Less than high school	1	1	1	0	0	0	0	0	3
High school	1	4	5	4	3	3	1	1	22
Some college	2	5	6	8	6	5	2	4	38
BA degree	0	1	1	2	3	4	2	3	16
Graduate degree	0	0	1	1	1	1	1	2	7
Total	4	11	14	15	13	13	6	10	86

INCOMES OF MARRIED COUPLES, HUSBAND HAS A BACHELOR'S DEGREE (BY ICONS ON THE POSTER)

INCOME IN THOUSANDS OF DOLLARS

	$0–20	$20–40	$40–60	$60–80	$80–100	$100–125	$125–150	$▸150	Total
Less than high school	0	0	0	0	0	1	0	0	1
High school	1	1	1	1	1	1	1	2	9
Some college	0	1	2	2	3	3	2	4	17
BA degree	0	2	4	5	4	4	3	10	32
Graduate degree	1	1	0	1	2	2	2	4	13
Total	2	5	7	9	10	11	8	20	72

INCOMES OF MARRIED COUPLES, HUSBAND HAS A GRADUATE DEGREE (BY ICONS ON THE POSTER)

INCOME IN THOUSANDS OF DOLLARS

	$0–20	$20–40	$40–60	$60–80	$80–100	$100–125	$125–150	$▸150	Total
Less than high school	0	0	0	0	0	0	0	0	0
High school	0	1	1	0	0	1	0	1	4
Some college	0	0	1	1	1	1	1	2	7
BA degree	1	0	1	2	1	2	2	7	16
Graduate degree	0	1	1	1	2	2	2	10	19
Total	1	2	4	4	4	6	5	20	46

Appendix II

Suggestions for Classroom Use

THE POSTER PROVIDES AN OPPORTUNITY to involve students directly in developing social analysis. After a brief introduction about the meaning of the symbols and colors, students should be encouraged to study and discuss the poster in groups of six to ten.

The first tendency is to find one's family on the poster, which may lead to the negative dynamic of students' comparing themselves and boasting about their relative status. This should be discouraged by having each student write *anonymously* the occupations of his or her parents and family income. The teacher can put this information on the blackboard and try to focus the discussion on the class taken as a whole rather than on individual circumstances. Even this may create problems, though: students may not know their family's income, and parents may question the validity of a classroom exercise that has their children coming home asking potentially sensitive questions.

That young people have little understanding of how high various living expenses run—another potential problem—can be turned to advantage by having them create family budgets as an initial exercise. To make up worksheets, teachers can consult the Consumer Expenditure Survey to find how much households at different income levels spend on twenty-five different types of purchases.

If a teacher does decide to poll the class anonymously, an income line from $0 to $300,000 can be drawn on the blackboard and an X used to mark off each student's family income. Then the distribution of the class can be compared to the shape of the poster or one of the graphs in the text. In most cases, the class's distribution will be much more concentrated than that of society at large. Depending on the results, the teacher can draw the appropriate conclusions. For example, most wealthy suburban communities consider themselves to be "upper middle class." They may be shocked to see that incomes in the $100,000–$250,000 range put them in rather limited company in relation to the whole population. The counterexample of a class from a poor neighborhood should be treated with care so as to avoid feelings of shame at placing low on the poster.

Once the class has developed a sense of itself, other exercises can involve picking different parts of town and fitting typical families from those places on the poster. Another possibility involves assigning six different households from different parts of the poster to separate groups of students. Each group can then be responsible for describing in greater depth the social conditions of that household.

Most of these exercises involve focusing on the vertical dimension of the poster. To emphasize the horizontal aspect, one can look at a given income range and compare the various households that make it up. In fact, families with the same income often live quite differently, with different expectations and lifestyles. Once again, students can learn more about society by actively studying its diversity. Other projects can target specific subgroups: retired people, women, blacks, one of the occupational categories, and so on. Tracing paper can be used to mark the appropriate figures, and then the pattern of X's on the tracing paper can be compared with the shape of the poster or to other traced shapes.

Other projects can focus on groups—for example, union workers—that may not be identified on the poster; students will have to ascertain which poster figures would be the appropriate match for the studied group.

Another possibility is to make international comparisons or comparisons over time. The class may wish to construct a picture of the United States in 1950, 1900, and 1850. Here, the problem of data availability becomes quite difficult because the decennial censuses (available in many large libraries) contain little detailed economic information before 1950. Some information is available, though, and doing original library research may be challenging. A good place to begin is the census's *Historical Statistics: Colonial Times to 1970*. Should a teacher try this exercise, it will quickly become clear how much information is necessary to construct a picture as complete as that presented on the poster. For other countries, the United Nations publishes a series of data books, and individual national reports may be obtained through consulates or interlibrary loan. Again, data availability will be limited.

These suggestions are only a starting point in the effort to involve students in caring about their social environment and trying to understand it. Within each exercise, there can be discussion of why things have developed in this fashion—particularly in the case of historical comparisons. All of this opens the door to questions about politics and citizenship. Thus, one can try to figure out which social groups support which party, push for new legislation, or take part in other forms of social action, such as demonstrations and forming organizations.

All of these activities will be possible if the students become involved with the poster and learn to identify history and social relations as tangible rather than abstract. By making one set of statistics accessible, the poster can heighten curiosity and give a sense of power to students to investigate other areas because they have a new way to understand them.

Appendix III

Other Published Works of the Author

"America Goes to College: The Hidden Promise of Higher Education in the Postindustrial Service Economy." With Anthony Carnevale. Georgetown Center on Education and Workforce, 2014.

"Blinder Baloney: Today's Scare Talk of Job Outsourcing Is Grossly Exaggerated." With William Dickens. *The International Economy,* October 2007.

"Certificates: The Gateway to Gainful Employment and College Degrees." With Anthony Carnevale. Georgetown Center on Education and Workforce, June 2012.

"The Challenge of Measuring Earnings Mobility and Career Paths in the United States." *Indicators: The Journal of Social Health* 1, no. 4 (2002): 73–98.

"The College Payoff: Education, Occupations, and Lifetime Earnings." With Anthony Carnevale. Georgetown Center on Education and Workforce, September 2011.

"Does Productivity Growth Still Benefit Working Americans? Unraveling the Income Growth Mystery to Determine How Much Median Incomes Trail Productivity Growth." The Information Technology and Innovation Foundation, June 2007.

"Inequality in the New High-Skilled Service Economy." With Anthony Carnevale. In *Unconventional Wisdom: New Perspectives in Economics,* ed. Jeff Madrick. Century Foundation Press.

Rebound: How America Will Emerge Stronger After the Financial Crisis. New York: St. Martin's Press, 2010.

"Socioeconomic Status, Race/Ethnicity, and Selective College Admissions." With Anthony Carnevale. In *America's Untapped Resource: Low-Income Students in Higher Education,* ed. Richard Kahlenberg. Century Foundation Press, 2003.

Still a Man's Labor Market: The Long-Term Earnings Gap. With Heidi Hartmann. Institute for Women's Policy Research, 2004. Reprinted in a condensed version as "The Long-Term Gender Gap," *Challenge* 47, no. 5 (2004): 30–50.

"Talking Past the Middle." *Challenge,* January 2007. A version of this article was the centerpiece of "Debating the Middle," organized by the editors of the *American Prospect* (http://www.prospect.org/cs/debates_chat).

"The Undereducated American." With Anthony Carnevale. Georgetown Center on Education and Workforce, June 2011.

"Ups and Downs: Does the American Economy Still Promote Upward Mobility?" With Scott Winship. Pew Economic Mobility Project, June 2009.

"The Value of a College Degree." *Change: The Magazine of Higher Learning* 45, no. 6 (2013): 24–33.